THE GUINNESS BOOK OF
ALMOST EVERYTHING YOU DIDN'T NEED TO KNOW ABOUT

THE MOVIES

Patrick Robertson

GUINNESS BOOKS

EDITOR: Honor Head
DESIGN AND LAYOUT: Michael Morey

© Patrick Robertson and Guinness Superlatives Ltd, 1986

Published in Great Britain by Guinness Superlatives Ltd,
33 London Road, Enfield, Middlesex

Typeset in 9/10 ITC Cheltenham Light
by Fakenham Photosetting Ltd, Fakenham, Norfolk
Printed and bound in Great Britain by R. J. Acford, Chichester, Sussex

'Guinness' is a registered trade mark of Guinness Superlatives Ltd
British Library Cataloguing in Publication Data

Robertson, Patrick
    The Guinness book of almost everything
    you didn't need to know about movies.–
    (Guinness oddfax)
    1. Moving-pictures–History
    I. Title
    791.43′09   PN1993.5.A1

    ISBN 0–85112–481–X

Patrick Robertson has had a passion for the movies
which began at the age of three when he was taken to
see *For Me and My Gal* on a wet afternoon in Lyme
Regis in 1943. In his spare time he runs a props hire
business, supplying vintage magazines, comics and
newspapers for set dressing in film and television
productions. He is also Chairman of the Ephemera
Society and author of *The Shell Book of Firsts* and
the *Guinness Book of Film Facts and Feats*.

CONTENTS

ONCE UPON A TIME

□□□□□□□□□□□□□□□□□□□□□□□

LUCKY BREAKS

Millions of pretty girls and handsome young men have dreamed of being picked out of the crowd by a movie director and signed to instant stardom. For most stars the road to fame and fortune was the more conventional one of drama school and years of playing stock. Sometimes, though, chance lends a hand. Here are some of those occasions.

☆ **Janet Leigh** was a psychology student when MGM star Norma Shearer happened to see a photo of her at a ski lodge in Northern California where her parents were employed. Miss Shearer took it to the studio, with the result that her protégée was given a role in *The Romance of Rosy Ridge* (US 47).

☆ **Ida Lupino** tagged along when her mother, actress Connie Emerald, attended an audition for *Her First Affaire* (GB 33). Mother was turned down as too old for the role of a provocative teenager, but her daughter, then aged 15 and strikingly beautiful, was given the part instead.

☆ **Jean-Pierre Léaud**, *enfant gaté* of Truffaut's Antoine Doinel films, won his first role at the age of 14 playing the lead in *The 400 Blows* (Fr 59) by answering an advertisement in *France-Soir*.

☆ **Rita Tushingham** was working as a bit part player and odd job girl for £1 a week at Liverpool Rep when she answered a newspaper advertisement for a working class northern girl to play the lead in Tony Richardson's *A Taste of Honey* (GB 61).

☆ The first American actress to achieve screen stardom without any prior stage experience was 17-year-old **Mae Marsh**, a salesgirl with a New York department store. One day she dropped into the Biograph Studios to see her sister, Marguerite Loveridge, and was spotted by D. W. Griffith, who had a casting problem because none of his contract players would consent to play the lead in *Man's Genesis* (US 12) with naked legs. Mae had no such inhibitions when Griffith offered her the part and the pretty barefoot girl made such an impression that she achieved instant stardom.

☆ **Gina Lollobrigida**, an art student in Rome, was stopped on the street by director Mario Costa. She let loose a torrent of abuse about men who accost defenceless girls and only when she paused for breath was he able to explain that he wanted to screen test her for *Elisir d'Amore* (It 46). She won the part.

☆ **Alan Dwan** was paying a visit to friends when he happened to spot the 13-year-old **Carole Lombard** clowning about in the next door neighbour's yard. He was looking for a lively tomboy to play the hero's daughter in *A Perfect Crime* (US 21) and signed her for the part.

*Ida Lupino's mother auditioned for this role in **Her First Affaire**, but it was her daughter who got the job.*

*Rita Tushingham was earning £1 a week in rep before she won the starring role in **A Taste of Honey** opposite Murray Melvin by answering a newspaper advertisement.*

☆ **Ellen Burstyn** secured her first major screen role in **Tropic of Cancer** (US 69), on the strength of a political speech director Joseph Strick heard her making in California.

☆ Another star whose oratory won him his first role—and in a silent film at that—was **Monte Blue**. He was a day labourer on the Fine-Arts lot and a union militant when D. W. Griffith happened to see him haranguing his workmates about some capitalist iniquity. The maestro gave him a major part as the French revolutionary leader Danton in **Orphans of the Storm** (US 22).

☆ **Greer Garson** got her start in Hollywood because MGM chief Louis B. Mayer went to see a straight play she was acting in called **Old Music**–under the misapprehension it was a musical. He did not get himself the singer he was looking for, but he unleashed oceans of tears by signing the star of some of MGM's four and five handkerchief-class weepies.

☆ **Pola Negri** did not wait to be chosen for the movies. She made her debut at the age of 20 in a film she had written and financed herself, **Love and Passion** (Pol 14). The rest of the films she made in her 50 year screen career tended to be on these same two themes.

☆ **Bibi Andersson** made her screen debut in a soap commercial. It was her good fortune that the director happened to be one Ingmar Bergman–leading to starring roles in masterpieces like **The Seventh Seal** (Swe 57), **Wild Strawberries** (Swe 57) and **Persona** (Swe 66).

☆ Perhaps the most ingenious ruse for breaking into movies was engineered by **Marsha Hunt**. Two friends of hers succeeded in placing a story with the *Los Angeles Times* to the effect that she was Hollywood's No 1 model– a total fabrication–with the additional information that she had positively no interest in a movie career. By noon four studios had called her with offers. She decided on Paramount, making her debut in **Virginia Judge** (US 35).

☆ **George Raft** began his career as a petty mobster whose ambition was to become a Mister Big. Sent as a protection racket heavy to extort money out of night club queen Texas Guinan, he succumbed instead to her offer of a part in her autobiopic **Queen of the Night Clubs** (US 29). Raft duly became a big time gangster– but only on screen.

☆ Archetypal flapper girl **Colleen Moore** won her first screen role in **The Big Boy** (US 17) as a favour granted for a favour received. Her uncle, an influential businessman, pulled strings to get D. W. Griffith's **Intolerance** (US 16) past the censors. In return the great director gave the screen-struck 15-year-old a chance in movies. She was to become the embodiment of the 20s image, her bobbed hair and short skirts imitated throughout the western world.

☆ **Clark Gable** was working as a telephone repair man when he met drama coach Josephine Dillon–he came to mend her phone. Despite the fact she was 14 years older than him, Gable broke off his engagement to another girl and married her. She trained him and won him his first roles as a bit player in such films as **The Merry Widow** (US 25), **The Plastic Age** (US 25) and **North Star** (US 25).

☆ Fifteen-year-old **Loretta Young** answered the telephone when director Mervyn Le Roy rang her big sister, Polly Ann Young, wanting her for a role in **Naughty**

But Nice (US 27). Polly Ann was away and Loretta found herself on the first step to stardom.

☆ Many would-be stars tried to catch the eye of the moguls by getting their scantily clad bodies onto a magazine cover. One of the few for whom it worked was **Ava Gardner**. She had been under contract to MGM for months without getting near a set. Then her picture appeared on the cover of the forces' paper *Stars and Stripes* and compelled the attention of studio chief Louis B Mayer. His first instruction was to find her and sign her. On being told he already 'owned' the feline beauty, Mayer ordered that the studio put her to work right away.

☆ Another cover girl who made a rapid rise to fame and fortune was **Lauren Bacall**. Her portrait adorning *Harper's Bazaar* was spotted by Howard Hawks and overnight stardom followed when he cast the sultry 19-year-old opposite Humphrey Bogart in **To Have or Have Not** (US 44). Marriage to Bogey followed the next year.

☆ **Fatty Arbuckle** got his first break due to a blocked drain. A plumber's mate, he was summoned to unblock Mack Sennett's pipes one day in 1913 and the producer immediately offered the 266 lbs fat boy a job in his Keystone Kops comedies.

☆ **Sonja Henie**, triple ice skating gold medallist in the 1928, 1932 and 1936 Olympics, was unable to persuade Hollywood producers that she was worth her asking price of $75,000 a picture until she hired an ice rink in Los Angeles to give a practical demonstration of her audience pull. She was a sell-out and Darryl Zanuck risked the

Fatty Arbuckle (far right) was a 266 lbs plumber's mate before he got his first break in movies in 1913. By 1919 he was Hollywood's highest paid star with a $1million contract, but only two years later his career ended as abruptly as it began when scandal made him the first star to be blacklisted by the studios.

unprecedented fee for an untried acting talent by casting her in ***One in a Million*** (US 36) opposite Adolphe Menjou–it too was a sell-out and Henie an instant star. Within two years she was Hollywood's highest paid performer at $16,000 a week.

☆ Everyone who has ever worked at a movie studio, in however humble a capacity, must have dreamed of being spotted by a famous director. It happened to props man Marion Morrison, who was loading furniture on to a truck one day in 1928 when he attracted the attention of Raoul Walsh. A change of name and ten years of hard graft in B movies led to stardom for **John Wayne.**

☆ **Olivia de Havilland** represents one of the very few true-life examples of the old showbiz cliche of the understudy who walks on to the stage an unknown and leaves it a star. On stand-by in Max Reinhardt's Hollywood Bowl production of ***A Midsummer Night's Dream***, she had to fill in as Hermia on the opening night. When the

Reinhardt production was transferred to screen in Warner Bros' 1935 film, she made her movie debut in the same role.

☆ **Shirley Maclaine** also fulfilled the understudy's dream of stardom. The night that Carol Haney, star of ***The Pyjama Game***, hurt her ankle and Miss Maclaine had to go on in her place was by chance the same night that producer Hal Wallis was in the audience. He signed her and loaned her out for her screen debut in Hitchcock's ***The Trouble with Harry*** (US 55).

☆ **Carole Landis** got her first starring role, in Hal Roach's ***One Million B.C.*** (US 40), by running barefoot down a studio street set to a telephone pole and back. The test was devised by D. W. Griffith, then working for Roach as an assistant, to find a girl who could move like a gazelle. Fifty other girls had raced down the street shoeless, but Landis was the only one who could run with the rhythm of a born athlete.

☆ **Judy Garland**'s contract with MGM was a mistake. Louis B.

Mayer saw the 14-year-old Judy and 15-year-old Deanna Durbin in a singing short called ***Every Sunday*** (US 36) and told an aide to 'Sign up that singer–the flat one'. Durbin, despite the quality of her voice, could sound a trifle flat on occasion. The aide misheard, thinking that Mayer had said 'the fat one', and signed pudgy little Miss Garland. Deanna Durbin went off to Universal instead, where her pictures earned a tidy $100 million over the next decade.

☆ **Rock Hudson** was a postman who had the good fortune to have agent Henry Willson on his regular round. Willson, impressed by his looks, learning that he had performed in school plays, and told that he did not like being a postman, arranged for Hudson to meet director Raoul Walsh, for whom he made his debut in ***Fighter Squadron*** (US 48).

☆ **Lana Turner** was not discovered at Schwab's Drug Store, as legend has it, but at Currie's Ice Cream Parlor, opposite Hollywood High School, where the 15-year-old was a pupil. The talent scout was Billy Wilkerson of ***The Hollywood Reporter*** and he vouches for the fact that she was indeed sipping a soda at the time. He took her to the Zeppo Marx Agency, who secured her a bit part in ***They Won't Forget*** (US 37)–sipping soda in a drugstore.

☆ Chance seldom has a role to play in the movie debuts of today's television-trained stars, but just occasionally a complete unknown still gets the fabled lucky break. France's new teenage star **Sandrine Bonnaire** answered an ad for extras to appear in Maurice Pialat's ***A Nos Amours*** (Fr 83). To her astonishment she was offered the lead instead. The picture won the César award for 'Best Film' and Sandrine's performance won her acclaim from critics and public alike.

○○○○○○○○○○○○○○○○○○○○○○○○○

FACES IN THE CROWD

These stars started their screen career as extras:

Theda Bara (1914)
Richard Barthelmess (1913)
Michael Caine (1953)
Gary Cooper (1925)
Marlene Dietrich (1922)
Clint Eastwood (1954)
Clark Gable (1924)
Janet Gaynor (1926)
John Gilbert (1915)
Paulette Goddard (1929)
Stewart Granger (1929)
Jean Harlow (1927)
Hedy Lamarr (1930)
Harold Lloyd (1912)
Sophia Loren (1950)
Peter Lorre (1929)
Joel McCrea (1923)
Fred MacMurray (1930)
Adolphe Menjou (1912)
Robert Mitchum (1943)
Marilyn Monroe (1947)
Roger Moore (1945)
David Niven (1935)
Ramon Novarro (1916)
Merle Oberon (1930)
Fernando Rey (1939)
Norma Shearer (1920)
Simone Signoret (1942)
Erich von Stroheim (1914)
Constance Talmadge (1914)
Rudolph Valentino (1914)
Michael Wilding (1929)
Loretta Young (1927)

Elizabeth Taylor also worked as an extra, but only *after* attaining stardom. She appears unbilled in crowd scenes in ***Quo Vadis*** (US 51) and ***Anne of the Thousand Days*** (GB 69).

FIRST THINGS FIRST

FAMOUS FIRSTS ...

☆ **The first motion picture film** was ***Traffic Crossing Leeds Bridge***, taken by French-born Louis Aimé Augustin Le Prince in October 1888. Le Prince disappeared, together with his projector, on a train from Dijon to Paris in September 1890. The mystery was never explained and he was never seen again.

☆ **The first film studio in the world** was Thomas Edison's **Black Maria**, a frame building covered in black roofing-paper, built at the Edison Laboratories in West Orange, New Jersey, and completed at a cost of $637.67 on 1 February 1893. Here Edison made short vaudeville act films for use in his Kinetoscope, a peep-show machine designed for amusement arcades. The building was so constructed that it could be revolved to face the direction of the sun.

☆ **The first film presented publicly on a screen** was ***Departure of the Workers of the Lumière Factory***, shown before members of the Société d'Encouragement pour l'Industrie Nationale by Auguste and Louis Lumière at 44 rue de Rennes, Paris, on 22 March 1895. The Lumière brothers gave their first show before a paying audience at the Grand Café, 14 Boulevard des Capucines, Paris on 28 December the same year.

☆ **The first western** was ***Kit Carson***, directed by Wallace McCutcheon for the American Mutoscope & Biograph Co. and filmed on location in the Adirondack Mountains of New York State on 8 September 1903.

☆ **The first full length feature film** in the world was an hour long Australian production titled ***The Story of the Kelly Gang***, shot on location in various parts of Victoria by Charles Tait at a total cost of £450 and premiered in Melbourne on 24 December 1906. This was some six years earlier than the first feature-length films made in America and Britain.

☆ **The first purpose-built cinema** was the **Cinéma Omnia Pathé**, Boulevard Montmatre, Paris, opened on 1 December 1906. It was also the first cinema with a raked floor so that everyone could see above the heads in front.

☆ **The first stars to have their names publicised** – a practice the producers resisted in case their $5 a day performers got big-headed and asked for more – were **Florence Lawrence** in America, **Henny Porten** in Germany and **Asta Nielsen** in Denmark, all three in 1910. First to become an international superstar with the salary to prove it – the producers' worst fears were quickly realised – was **Asta Nielsen**, who was earning $80,000 a year by 1912. This was six times the salary of the then highest paid star in America.

Everyone knows that Al Jolson was the first actor to speak in a feature movie, **The Jazz Singer** *in 1927. But what about the first actress? Eugenie Besserer took the honours, playing Jolson's mum, and spoke all of 13 words to ensure her screen immortality.*

☆ **The first studio in Hollywood** was the **Nestor Studio**, established in a derelict roadhouse on Sunset Boulevard by the Centaur Co. in October 1911. The decision to make films in this outlying district of Los Angeles depended on the toss of a coin. Centaur's chief director, Al Christie, wanted to move production from New Jersey to California, but company president David Horsley favoured a move to Florida. They agreed on a heads-or-tails selection and Christie won.

☆ **The first full-length feature in natural colour** was *The World, the Flesh and the Devil*, made in Britain in Kinemacolor in 1914. The acting and direction were generally reckoned to be execrable, but the colour impressive.

☆ **The first full-length cartoon feature film** was not a Walt Disney production, but an Argentine movie called **El Apostol** made by Don Frederico Valle in 1917. Nor did the first feature-length cartoon talkie come from Disney–that was from Argentina too, Quirino Cristiani's **Peludopolis** of 1931.

☆ **The first sound-on-film talkie** was **The Arsonist**, a short drama made in the Tri-Ergon process and presented at the Alhambra cinema in Berlin on 17 September 1922. It starred Erwin Baron, who played seven out of the nine parts.

☆ **The first feature-length talkie** was Alan Crosland's **The Jazz Singer**, premiered at the Warner Theatre on Broadway on 6 October 1927. Warner Bros intended the sound to be confined to music and songs, but Al Jolson ad libbed some speech, beginning with the famous words, 'Wait a minute! Wait a minute! You ain't heard nothin' yet'. It gave the picture such a lift that the two spoken sequences were kept in. For the record, there were 354 words spoken in total, 340 of them by Jolson, 13 by Eugenie Besserer (playing his mother), and one by Warner Oland (as his father)–'Stop!'

☆ **The first musical** (with an original score) was MGM's **The Broadway Melody**, premiered at Grauman's Chinese Theater in Hollywood on 1 February 1929. Starring Bessie Love, it included George M. Cohan's hit **Give My Regards to Broadway**.

☆ **The first cartoon talkie** was Paul Terry's **Dinner Time**, premiered on 1 September 1928. Walt Disney, whose first Mickey Mouse cartoon, **Steamboat Willie**, was to be released a few weeks later, described his rival's pioneer venture as 'a lot of racket and nothing else'.

☆ **The first feature film in three-colour Technicolor** was Rouben Mamoulian's **Becky Sharp**, starring Sir Cedric Hardwicke and Miriam Hopkins. On its release in 1935, *Liberty* said the performers looked like 'boiled salmon dipped in mayonnaise'.

☆ **The first feature-length talking picture in 3-D** was Sante Bonaldo's 1936 production **Nozze vagabonde**, starring Leda Gloria and Ermes Zacconi. The Italian film was too far in advance of its time; Hollywood only took to 3-D in 1953.

☆ **Cinemascope** also arrived in Hollywood in 1953 and was even more belated. The idea had been developed as early as 1927, when French inventor Henri Chrétien developed his anamorphic Hypergonar system. Fox bought the patent rights in 1952 and the first Cinemascope feature film, **The Robe**, was premiered at Grauman's on 24 September 1953.

☆ **The first movie based on a TV series** was the 1954 crime thriller **Dragnet**, starring Jack Webb as Sergeant Joe Friday, the role he had created in the NBC television series which had then been running three years and was to continue till 1959. In 1969 the movie of the TV show was remade as a television movie.

☆ **The first full-length made-for-televison movie** was **High Tor**, top-lining Bing Crosby, which was networked coast to coast in America on 10 March 1956 and is chiefly notable for the fact that it featured Julie Andrews in her American screen debut. *Films in*

*Nearly every major movie nowadays is released in Dolby Stereo. It all began with Ken Russell's **Lisztomania** in 1975, with Roger Daltrey as Franz Liszt.*

Review's critic commented: 'The commercials were a welcome relief '.

☆ **The first video films** were available for hire from Sears, Roebuck in the USA in 1972 and included **Stagecoach** (US 39), **Hamlet** (GB 48), **High Noon** (US 52), **The Bridge on the River Kwai** (GB 57), **Cactus Flower** (US 69) and **The Anderson Tapes** (US 71). They were for showing on the Avco Cartavision video player, which retailed for $1,600. The first video films to be put on sale were 50 Fox productions issued on tape by Magnetic Video at $50 each in 1977.

☆ **The first film released in Dolby Stereo** was Ken Russell's

1975 British production *Lisztomania*, starring Roger Daltrey. The Dolby sound system, which 'reproduces the silence as accurately as the sound', was developed by American-born Ray Dolby in an old dressmaking factory in Fulham.

☆ **The first commercial play-off of a movie with digital sound** took place at the Plitt Century Plaza Theater in Century City, California over a four-week period during February/March 1985. A specially recorded version of Disney's 1941 cartoon feature *Fantasia* was used for the presentation, with the sound emanating from a digital audio playback unit synchronised with the projector. The process allows exact reproduction of sound.

☆ **The first feature film shot in black-and-white to be converted to full colour** was the 1942 James Cagney biopic of George M. Cohan *Yankee Doodle Dandy*. The special prints with their computer applied colour were released by MGM on 4 July 1985.

𝄇▢▢▢▢▢▢▢▢▢▢▢▢▢▢▢▢▢▢▢𝄆

... AND NOT SO FAMOUS FIRSTS

☆ **The first ever leading role in a movie**, the part of Mary in *The Execution of Mary Queen of Scots* (US 95), was played in drag by a gentleman called Mr R. L. Thomas.

☆ **The first screen kiss** and the **first film review** were both engendered by the same movie, *The Widow Jones* (US 96). The kiss was a big slobbery one implanted on the receptive lips of May Irwin by John Rice. The review, in *The Chap Book* for 15

June 1896, consisted of the words 'absolutely disgusting'.

☆ **The first film to be made on location overseas** was the Urban Trading Co.'s *Hiawatha* (GB 03), directed in 20 scenes by ex-Boer cameraman Joe Rosenthal, and made in Ontario with a cast composed entirely of Red Indians drawn from the Ojibway tribe.

☆ **The first colour western**, a 1911 Kinemacolor production titled *Fate*, was directed by a Dutchman (Theo Bouwmeester), set in Texas and filmed in Sussex!

☆ **The first ballistic custard pie** was discharged by Mabel Normand in the direction of Fatty Arbuckle in *A Noise from the Deep* (US 13). It was a true case of the biter bit, because in subsequent pictures Mabel was generally the recipient of Arbuckle's pies. He had an unerring aim and an extraordinary physical dexterity that enabled him to hurl two pies at once in opposite directions.

☆ **The first occasion on which a film was used as evidence in court** was on 4 March 1914 during the trial of Samuel London, charged with producing a lewd and immoral picture, to wit *The Inside of the White Slave Traffic* (US 13), and Harry C. Bohn, proprietor of the Park Theatre, New York, charged with giving an immoral exhibition. In a court in General Sessions, Judge Edward Swann acceded to the assistant DA's request that the complete film be shown in evidence and himself applied to the Department of Water, Gas and Electricity for a license to turn the courtroom into a cinema.

☆ **The first make-up specifically for on-screen use** was Supreme Greasepaint, introduced by Polish immigrant Max Factor in 1914. The need for special make-up was dictated by the increasing use of artificial lighting for filming from 1912 onwards. Freckles and skin blemishes photographed black, pink cheeks a murky grey, and skin tones a deathly white.

☆ **The first performer to achieve simultaneous premieres on stage and screen** was Marie Dressler, who opened in *A Mix Up* at the 39th Street Theater on the same night, Monday 30 December 1914, that her feature length comedy *Tillie's Punctured Romance*, in which she starred together with Charlie Chaplin and Mabel Normand, had its world premiere at the New York Theatre.

☆ Contrary to popular belief, **the first star to appear on screen in the nude** was not Hedy Lamarr in the 1933 Czech film *Extase*. In fact there were two pioneer movie nudies who starred in different films released in the same week in October 1916: Australian-born ex-swimming champion Annette Kellerman in *Daughter of the Gods* and winsome 16-year-old newcomer June Caprice in *The Ragged Princess*. Hedy Lamarr did, however, score another notable first in *Extase*–it was the first film in which the sex act is depicted.

☆ **The first leading lady to wear trousers on screen** as an article of feminine apparel was Myrna Loy in *What Price Beauty* (US 24).

☆ **The first footprints outside Grauman's Chinese Theater in Hollywood** were Norma Talmadge's on 18 May 1927. Legend has it that she stepped on the wet cement by accident, thereby giving Sid Grauman the idea for his celebrated and still continuing publicity stunt.

☆ **The first film to be flown across the Atlantic** for overseas release was Fritz Lang's *Spies*, from Germany to the USA in 1928.

☆ **The first film shown on television** was British Sound Productions' *The Bride*, featuring George Robey, which was transmitted from the Baird Television Studios in Long Acre on 19 August 1929. The first film made for television was a comedy titled *The Early Bird Catches the Worm*, made by Commerz-Film of Berlin for the Reichs-Rundfunkgesellschaft in 1930.

☆ **The first film in which people are depicted performing the natural functions** was the Soviet production *Earth* of 1930. Like most Russian films of the period it is about tractors, and during the scene in question one of them runs out of water and peasants urinate into the radiator. Many years were to pass before the bowel action was depicted on screen and perhaps not surprisingly it was in an Australian movie, *The Office Picnic* of 1972, in which a character is seen seated on the lavatory with the door open. In a French film of the same year, *La Grande Bouffe*, Michel Piccoli perishes in his own excrement as a result of over-eating.

☆ **The first profanity to be uttered on screen** was the word 'damn' by Emma Dunn in *Blessed Event* (US 32).

*Dancing pigs in Victorian dress to uplift the toiling masses: **The Tales of Beatrix Potter** was the first British film released in Red China.*

☆ **The first Hollywood movie in an urban setting to be filmed entirely on location** was Universal's 1948 ***The Naked City***, a murder story located in the teeming streets of New York. Directed by Jules Dassin, the film contained no studio sets, even the interior scenes, such as those in a police station, being taken in real locations.

☆ **The first major screen actor to establish a reputation on television** before entering films–nowadays the classic route to Hollywood–was Charlton Heston. During the late 1940s he played Antony in ***Julius Caesar*** and Heathcliff in ***Wuthering Heights***, among other significant roles in TV plays, and these performances attracted the attention of Paramount, leading to his large screen debut in ***Dark City*** (US 50) when he was 27.

☆ **The first screen tests to be conducted in the nude** (porno movies excepted) were for the femme leads in ***Four for Texas*** (US 63), which starred Ursula Andress and Anita Ekberg. Those reluctant to be tested need not have worried; the censor clipped all the nude scenes.

☆ **The first film with full frontal female nudity**, including pubic hair, to be shown in British cinemas was the 1966 Swedish picture ***Hugs and Kisses***. Initially the British Board of Film Censors insisted that the offending scene, a 15 second shot of the heroine looking at her naked body in a mirror, should be cut, but after the film was passed intact by a number of local authorities, with no public outcry, the censor relented and a certificate was granted in 1968. In the meantime ***If*** (GB 68), which had a scene of the housemaster's wife wandering around the school dormitories nude, had become the first such film passed by the Board.

☆ **The first British film released in Red China** was ***The Tales of Beatrix Potter*** (GB 71) in 1972. What the toiling masses made of dancing pigs wearing Victorian costume is unrecorded.

☆ **The first film containing a scene of sexual intercourse to be passed fit for juvenile (accompanied) audiences** in Britain was *Siddartha* (US 72).

☆ **The first Soviet made western** was Vladamir Vainshtok's *Armed and Very Dangerous* (USSR 78), with locations in Czechoslovakia, Rumania and southern Russia standing in for tumbleweed country. The identity of the villain is not revealed until the very end; not unexpectedly, it turns out to be the chief capitalist-exploiter in town.

⌷⌷⌷⌷⌷⌷⌷⌷⌷⌷⌷⌷⌷⌷⌷⌷⌷⌷⌷⌷⌷

FIRST KISS

For some child stars, the first screen kiss represented the threshold of adult stardom; for others, sadly, it marked the waning point of a career that failed. Here are the films in which the movies' most famous little girls first tasted romance–and who bestowed the kiss.

☆ **Petula Clark** (16) by Jimmy Hanley in *Don't Ever Leave Me* (GB 49)

Deanna Durbin (18) by Robert Stack in *First Love* (US 39)

Jodie Foster (15) by Bernard Giaradeau in *Moi, Fleur Bleue* (Fr 77)

Margaret O'Brien (14) by Allen Martin Jr in *Her First Romance* (US 51)

Tatum O'Neal (16) by Jeffrey Byron in *International Velvet* (GB 78)

Brooke Shields (14) by Christopher Atkins in *The Blue Lagoon* (US 80)

Elizabeth Taylor (14) by Marshall Thompson in *Cynthia* (US 46)

Shirley Temple (14) by Dickie Moore in *Miss Annie Rooney* (US 42).

⌷⌷⌷⌷⌷⌷⌷⌷⌷⌷⌷⌷⌷⌷⌷⌷⌷⌷⌷⌷⌷

LADIES FIRST

These are the women who were the first of their sex in various fields of film-making.

☆ **Camerawoman** Rosina Cianelli, who shot her first film, *Uma Transformista Original*, in Brazil in 1909.

☆ **Camerawoman** (newsreel) Dorothy Dunn became the first

Marshall Thompson may never have attained the heights of Hollywood stardom, but would he ever forget that he it was who gave Elizabeth Taylor her first screen kiss in **Cynthia**?

and only ever woman news cameraman when she joined the crew of **Universal Animated Weekly** in America c. 1918.

☆ **Camerawoman** (feature) Tamara Lobova, whose debut film was **Suvorov** (USSR 41).

☆ **Composer** Jadan Bai, whose first score was for **Talash-e-Huq** (India 35).

☆ **Composer** (Hollywood) Elizabeth Firestone, daughter of tyre magnate Harvey Firestone, who scored the Robert Montgomery comedy **Once More, My Darling** (US 47).

☆ **Director** Alice Guy, who began directing for Gaumont in Paris with **La Fée aux Choux** (Fr 1900).

☆ **Director** (feature) Lois Weber, whose first full-length feature was **The Merchant of Venice** (US 14).

☆ **Director** (talkie) Dorothy Arzner with **Manhattan Cocktail** (US 28).

☆ **Director-Writer-Star** Elaine May performed all three functions when she made **A New Leaf** (US 70).

☆ **Director-Producer-Writer-Star** Barbra Streisand on **Yentl** (GB 83).

☆ **Producer** Alice Guy, who produced **A Child's Sacrifice** starring 'The Solax Kid' (Magda Foy) for the Solax Co. of Fluhing, NY in 1910 and followed it up with some 300 other shorts in the next three years.

☆ **Producer** (feature) Countess Bubna, who produced a gangster movie set in New York called **The Definite Object** for the British company Eros Film in 1920.

☆ **Producer** (talkie) Elinor Glyn, the famous novelist, who

Barbra Streisand not only starred in **Yentl***, but directed, produced and wrote the movie as well.*

produced and directed **Knowing Men** in colour and different language versions, French and English, for the British company Talkicolor in 1929.

☆ **Production Chief** Sherry Lansing, who became Head of Production at 20th Century Fox and the industry's highest paid woman executive in 1981.

☆ **Screenwriter** (full-time) Anita Loos, who sold her first scenario, **The New York Hat**, to Biograph in 1912 and was engaged as a staff writer by the company's foremost director, D. W. Griffith.

☆ **Screenwriter to win Oscar** Frances Marion for **The Big House** (US 30), a prison drama starring Wallace Beery and Robert Montgomery.

☆ **Stuntwoman** Helen Gibson, who doubled for Helen Holmes in the long running serial **The Hazards of Helen**, starting in 1914.

WHAT'S IN A NAME?

MAKING A NAME FOR THEMSELVES

☆ The easiest way of acquiring a screen name is to change a single letter of the one you were born with: **Renee Asherson** (Ascherson); **Warren Beaty** (Beatty); **Dirk Bogarde** (Bogaerde); **Beulah Bondy** (Bondi); **Yul Brynner** (Bryner); **Madeleine Carroll** (O'Carroll); **Irene Dunne** (Dunn); **Curt Jurgens** (Juergens); **Vivien Leigh** (Vivian); **Dorothy Malone** (Maloney); **Gerard Philipe** (Philippe); **George Raft** (Ranft); **May Robson** (Robison); **Barbra** (Barbara) **Streisand**; **Ronald Squire** (Squirl); **Conrad Veidt** (Weidt).

☆ Another way of going about it is to change your christian name: Clarence/**Robert Cummings**; Virginia/**Bebe Daniels**; Ruth/ **Bette Davis**; Sari/**Zsa Zsa Gabor**; Norvell/**Oliver Hardy**; Leslie/**Bob Hope**; John/**Arthur Kennedy**; Julius/**Groucho Marx**; John/**Tim McCoy**; James/**David Niven**; Marilyn/**Kim Novak**; William/**Pat O'Brien**; Julia/**Lana Turner**; Hubert/**Rudy Vallee**; Adolf/ **Anton Walbrook**.

☆ Alternatively you could use your middle name as a first name: (William) **Clark Gable**; (Edward) **Montgomery Clift**; (Terence) **Steve McQueen**; (Patrick) **Ryan O'Neal**; (Eldred) **Gregory Peck**; (Ernestine) **Jane Russell**; (Edith) **Norma Shearer.**

☆ A number of stars adopted names from their mother's side of the family. **Monroe** was the name of Marilyn's maternal grandmother. **Jean Harlow** (Harlean Carpenter) took her mother's maiden name, as did **Simone Signoret** (Simone-Henriette-Charlotte Kaminker), **Rita Hayworth** (Margarita Cansino), **Gloria Grahame** (Gloria Hallward) and **Shelley Winters** (Shirley Schrift). **Broderick Crawford** took his first name from his mother, Helen Broderick. Fairbanks was the name of Doug's mother's first husband (his real surname was Ulman). **Joan Fontaine** (Joan de Havilland) assumed the name of her mother's second husband, though she was the daughter of the first. Sister **Olivia** kept her name unchanged.

☆ Rather less usual is using your christian name as a surname, but Malden Sekulovich did so when he became **Karl Malden** and Allen Stewart Konigsberg switched to **Woody Allen**.

☆ Some stars have been named after other stars: **Shirley Jones** was named after Shirley Temple and **Doris Day** after silent star Doris Kenyon. **Marilyn Monroe** (Norma Jean Baker) was given her first name by Fox talent scout Ben Lyon because of his admiration for Marilyn Miller. **Gilbert Roland** (Luis Alonso) made up his screen name from a composite of his two favourite stars–John Gilbert and Ruth Roland. **Dustin Hoffman**'s screen-struck mother named him after early cowboy star Dustin Farnum, and Austrian born screen siren of the 30s and 40s **Hedy Lamarr** (Hedwig Kiesler) took her Hollywood screen surname from a siren of the 20s, Barbara La Marr.

☆ Other stars took their names from characters in literature or characters they had played. **Bette Davis** (Ruth Davis) named herself after Balzac's *Cousin Bette*. **Barbara Stanwyck** (Ruby Stevens) was given her surname by Willard Mack after a character called Jane Stanwyck in the play *Barbara Frietchie*. **Gig Young** (Byron Barr) took the name of the character he played in *The Gay Sisters* (US 42), while **Bob Steele** (Robert North Bradbury) assumed his name from the role he played in *The Mojave Kid* (US 28) and former child star Dawn O'Day switched to **Anne Shirley** to play the heroine of that name in *Anne of Green Gables* (US 34). **James Craig** acquired his name after playing in **Craig's Wife** (US 36). **Cary Grant** (Archie Leach) borrowed his first name from the character Cary Lockwood he played in the New York stage production *Nikki* and **Michael Caine** (Maurice Micklewhite) took his surname not from that of a character but a film title–*The Caine Mutiny* (US 54). **Anouk Aimée** (Françoise Sorya) played a servant with that name when she made her screen debut in *La Maison la Mer* (Fr 47).

☆ A few stars even named themselves after places. Cowboy star emeritus **Tom Mix** hailed from Mix Run, Pa and **Bela Lugosi**, whose last name was really Blasko, from Lugos in Hungary. **Gary** (Frank) **Cooper** was named after his agent's hometown of Gary, Indiana. His own would hardly have been appropriate–he came from Helena, Montana.

☆ Quite a number of stars have shared the same name. While Spangler Arlington Brugh was sensible enough to change his name to the rather less singular **Robert Taylor**, the real Robert Taylor felt there was only room for one of them as he left his native Australia for stardom in London and Hollywood and shortened his first name to Rod. There was no such problem for the two Misses Gladys Smith, because one preferred to be known as **Mary Pickford** and the other decided to be **Alexis Smith**. **Vera Miles** would have been content to remain Vera Ralston, but for the fact there was already one in Hollywood, former skating champion Vera Hruba Ralston. Byron Barr thought his name sounded pretentious and changed it to **Gig Young**, whereupon another actor, looking for something dashing and romantic, adopted the name **Byron Barr**. Bernard Schwarz chose to be called **Tony Curtis**, while the real Tony Curtis became Italy's well-loved comedian **Toto**. American actor Bud Flanagan changed his name to **Dennis O'Keefe** and British actor Robert Winthrop altered his to **Bud Flanagan**. It was fortunate for **James Stewart** that his British namesake had already decided to change James Stewart into **Stewart Granger** before the other James Stewart headed for Hollywood.

☆ **Lili Damita** had her screen name conferred on her by a monarch. Holidaying at Biarritz in 1921 when she was 17, she attracted the attention of the King of Spain, who enquired after the *damita del maillo rojo (young lady in a red bathing dress)*.

☆ **Doris Day** (Doris von Kapellof) was given her screen surname by bandleader Barney Rapp, for whom she had sung *Day After Day*.

☆ Less romantic was **Carole Lombard**'s decision to name herself after the Carroll, Lombardi Pharmacy on Lexington and 65th in New York.

☆ **ZaSu Pitts**' curious first name, with its interpolated capital S, was compounded of the last syllable of her Aunt Eliza's name and the first of her Aunt Susan's.

☆ Gretchen **Young** had her first name changed to **Loretta** by Colleen Moore, who discovered her as a 14-year-old extra in ***Her Wild Oat*** (US 26). Loretta, said Miss Moore, was the name of 'the most beautiful doll I ever had'.

☆ **Judy Holliday** was born Judy Tuvim–*tuvim* in Hebrew means *holiday*.

☆ **Judy Garland** (Frances Gumm) borrowed her first name from the Hoagy Carmichael song *Judy*, while her surname came from the theatre pages of a Chicago Newspaper whose reviews were written by one Robert Garland. It was chosen by George Jessel, to whom the 11-year-old Miss Gumm had appealed for help after being billed as Glumm at the theatre where they were both appearing.

☆ **Wendy Barrie** (Marguerite Wendy Jenkins) was called Wendy after the character in J. M. Barrie's *Peter Pan* and took her surname from the playwright, who was her godfather. In later years she was to mix in less select company, even if it included godfathers–she became an intimate friend of gangster Bugsy Siegel.

☆ Joseph **Keaton** acquired the first name of **'Buster'** at the age of six when he fell downstairs and Harry Houdini, a family friend, remarked to his father: 'That was some buster your baby took!'

☆ **Jack Oakie** (Lewis Offield) was one–an Oakie from Muskogee, Oklahoma.

☆ **Groucho** (Julius) **Marx** took his first name from a comic strip character called Groucho Monk. Chico, Harpo and Gummo were other characters in the same strip, *Mager's Monks*.

☆ Another comic strip, titled *The Bingville Bugle*, was the favourite reading of young Harry **Crosby**, whose schoolmates soon invested him with the nickname **Bing**.

☆ **'Zero'** was also a school nickname, acquired by the unfortunate Master Samuel **Mostel** because he usually scored that number of marks.

☆ **Hoot Gibson**'s nickname (real name Edmund Gibson) was conferred on him in boyhood on account of his passion for hunting owls.

☆ **Stepin Fetchit**, the startled black manservant of innumerable Hollywood comedies, named himself after a racehorse which had obliged him by winning.

☆ **Rock Hudson** (Roy Scherer) had his screen name conferred on him by agent Henry Willson and it was topographical in origin, a compound of Rock of Gibraltar and the Hudson River in New York State.

Virginia Mayo was named after a horse, but not this one–hers was a pantomime horse.

☆ **Virginia Mayo** (Virginia Jones) named herself after a performing horse she acted feed to in vaudeville. The front and back legs of the animal were the two Mayo brothers.

□□□□□□□□□□□□□□□□□□□□□□□

STAR TITLES

When a performer's name was billed above the title, that meant real stardom. But an even greater accolade of fame is for a star's name to appear *in* the title–particularly when the star is not in the movie. (Where the title is marked with an asterisk, the star did appear.) Omitted from this list are star biopics and also titles containing the names of performers like Abbott and Costello who always played a fictitious version of themselves. The first title listed, therefore, is on account of Karloff rather than the comedy duo.

Abbott and Costello Meet the

Killer, Boris Karloff (US 48)*

Adolf and Marlene (W. Ger 77)–with Margit Carstensen as Marlene Dietrich

Bela Lugosi Meets a Brooklyn Gorilla (US 52)*

The Black Dragon Revenges the Death of Bruce Lee (HK 75)

Chaplin! Who Do You Cry (Jap 32)–porno

Charlie Chaplin and the Kung Fu Kid in Laughing Times (HK 81)

Charlie Chaplin Na Vitoscia (Bul 24)

Come Back to the 5 and Dime, Jimmy Dean, Jimmy Dean (US 82)

The Curse of Fred Astaire (US 84)

Dear Brigitte (US 65)*

F comme Fairbanks (Fr 75)

Garbo Talks (US 86)

Gary Cooper, Who Art in Heaven (Sp 81)

Ginger and Fred (It 86)

The Gracie Allen Murder Case (US 39)*

Happy Birthday, Marilyn! (Hun 81)–Yes, it does refer to MM

In Like Flynn (US 85)

Ist Eddy Polo Schuldig (Ger 28)*

The Kiss of Mary Pickford (USSR 26)*–shot clandestinely without the star knowing she was in it (see p. 119)

The Little Valentino (Hun 79)

The Man with Bogart's Face (US 80)

The Semester We Loved Kim Novak (Sp 80)

Shirley Temple se enamora (Mex 38)

Valentino Returns (US 86)
The Woman Who Married
Clark Gable (Ire 85)

Mae Murray was the 'Girl with the Bee-stung Lips'.

SOBRIQUETS

The American Beauty Katherine MacDonald, of whom it was said by one ungenerous critic that 'her acting ability is not to be classed with her beauty'.

The American Venus Esther Ralston

America's Favourite Lovebirds Charles Farrell and Janet Gaynor

America's Scream Queen Jeanne-Ann Birnkrant, who specialises in playing screaming, hysterical females

America's Sweetheart Mary Pickford

The Battling Bogarts Humphrey Bogart and first wife Mayo Methot, who lost him to Lauren Bacall

The Beard Monty Wooley

The Best Dressed Woman in the World Irene Castle

The Blonde Bombshell Betty Hutton

The Body Marie MacDonald, blonde beauty of the 40s

The Brazilian Bombshell Carmen Miranda

The Cat Simone Silva

The Champagne Blonde Evelyn Laye

The Chest George O'Brien

The Duke John Wayne–named after a pooch he owned as a boy

The Empress of Emotion Elissa Landi

The Feet Rita Moreno

The Fiddle and the Bow Laurel and Hardy

The First Gentleman of the Screen George Arliss

The First Lady of the Screen Norma Shearer

The Girl with the Bee-Stung Lips Mae Murray

The Girl with the $100,000 Legs silent star Cecilia Evans

The Girl with the Million Dollar Legs Betty Grable

The Girl with the Perfect Face Linda Darnell

The Goldwyn Girl Mae Marsh

The Great Profile John Barrymore

The Green-Eyed Goddess Jane Winton

The Handsomest Lovers on the Screen Kent Taylor and Evelyn Venable

The Handsomest Man in the World Francis X. Bushman

The Heart of America Marie Dressler

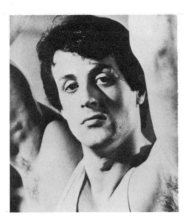

The Italian Stallion.

The Hero Brothers silent screen heroes Owen, Matt and Tom Moore

The Hunk Victor Mature

The Iceberg Anita Ekberg

The Ice Maiden Ursula Andress

The Iron Butterfly Loretta Young

The Italian Stallion Sylvester Stallone

The It Girl Clara Bow

The King of Hollywood Clark Gable

The King of the Cliff-Hangers Antonio Moreno

The King of the Cowboys Roy Rogers

The King of the Heavies Roy Batcroft, who played mean and dirty in 200 B westerns

The Lady with the Loveliest Legs in London Jesse Matthews

La Lollo Gina Lollobrigida

The Look Lauren Bacall

The Love Goddess Rita Hayworth

The Love Rouser Buddy Rogers

The Magnificent Wildcat Pola Negri

The Man of a Thousand Faces Lon Chaney

The Man You Love To Hate Erich von Stroheim

The Meanest Man in the World Jack Benny

The Mexican Spitfire Lupe Velez

The Military Heartburglar David Owell, English actor in early Hollywood usually cast in military roles

Mr Beefcake Victor Mature

Mr Hollywood Charles Watson, so dubbed by the USO in recognition of his battlefield tours during World War II

The Most Beautiful Chorus Girl in Hollywood Toby Wing

Ol' Blue Eyes Frank Sinatra

The Oomph Girl Ann Sheridan

The Orchid Lady of the Screen Corinne Griffith

The Platinum Blonde Jean Harlow

The Prince Consort Conrad Nagel

The Professional Virgin Doris Day

The Queen of Technicolor Maureen O'Hara

The Queen of the B's Claire Trevor

Queen of the Movies Myrna Loy

The Sex Kitten Brigitte Bardot

Sexpot of the Century Jane Russell

The Son of America Douglas Fairbanks

The Sweater Girl Lana Turner

The Thinking Man's Bardot Marie-France Pisier

The Thinking Woman's Crumpet Tom Conti

The Threat Lizabeth Scott

The Vagabond Lover Rudy Vallee

The Viennese Teardrop Luise Rainer

The Vitagraph Girl Florence Turner

The World's Greatest Female Tap Dancer Eleanor Powell

The World's Sweetheart Janet Gaynor

NOT STARRING

Often a role that appears to have been tailor made for a particular star was intended for someone else altogether.

☆ **George Jessel**, initial choice for the lead in *The Jazz Singer* (US 27), lost the opportunity to be the first star of a talking picture because he demanded an extra $10,000 for singing on top of the $30,000 Warner Bros offered him for the role. Next choice was **Eddie Cantor**, who turned down the role because he thought it could and should only be played by Jessel. Al Jolson upped the ante with a demand of $75,000 and a by then desperate Jack Warner capitulated.

☆ **Noel Coward** was Stanley Kubrick's first choice for the hapless child-lover in *Lolita* (GB 62), a role tackled with relish by James Mason, who considered it his best film.

☆ Stars practically queued up not to have to play the washed-up has-been opposite Judy Garland in *A Star Is Born* (US 54). Among those rejecting the role before James Mason took it on were **Humphrey Bogart**, **Cary Grant** (who first accepted, then backed out), **Gary Cooper**, **Marlon Brando** and **Montgomery Clift**.

☆ **Henry Fonda** turned down the part which won Peter Finch his posthumous Oscar in *Network* (US 76) as 'too hysterical'.

☆ **Robert Montgomery** was scheduled to play Clark Gable's Oscar winning role in *It Happened One Night* (US 34), but Columbia backed away at the last moment when MGM released another Montgomery picture, *Fugitive Lovers* (US 34), with a similar story-line. Instead MGM offered them Gable as a punishment for refusing a role opposite Joan Crawford.

☆ **Robert Redford** rejected the George Segal role in *Who's Afraid of Virginia Woolf* (US 66), the Dustin Hoffman role in *The Graduate* (US 67) and the John Cassavetes role in *Rosemary's Baby* (US 68)–all before he became a major star.

☆ Judy Garland secured the lead in *The Wizard of Oz* (US 39) only because Fox refused to loan **Shirley Temple** to MGM for the role. Shirley was the right age for the part of Dorothy–Judy was 17 playing a 9-year-old.

☆ **Cary Grant** was originally top-lined for *The Third Man* (GB 49) in the William Holden role; for *Sabrina* (US 54) in the Bogart role; and for *A Star Is Born* (US 54) in the James Mason role. He was also first choice for Professor Higgins in *My Fair Lady* (US 64).

☆ **Olivia de Havilland** was first choice for the role of Blanche, which won Vivien Leigh an Oscar, in *A Streetcar Named Desire* (US 51). **John Garfield** was offered the Brando role as Stanley

*Greer Garson replaced Norma Shearer as **Mrs Miniver** because Miss Shearer would not play a maternal role.*

Kowalski, but rejected it because he felt the male lead was much inferior to the female lead.

☆ **Vivien Leigh** was replaced by Elizabeth Taylor after having a breakdown on **Elephant Walk** (US 53), but did not disappear from the film altogether. Lynx-eyed Leigh fans have spotted her in a number of long shots which were not retaken.

☆ **Eli Wallach** was chosen for the Sinatra role in **From Here to Eternity** (US 53), but withdrew mysteriously without stating a reason, thereby fuelling the rumours that Sinatra had got the part through Mafia pressure.

☆ Betty Hutton got the chance to play what was undoubtedly her best role in **Annie Get Your Gun** (US 49) after **Judy Garland** had walked off the set halfway through shooting.

☆ **Vanessa Redgrave** backed out of **Georgy Girl** (GB 66) at the last moment, leaving the role open to sister Lynn.

☆ **Lee Marvin** and **Rod Steiger** both opted out of playing the role that conferred superstar status on George C. Scott in **Patton: Lust for Glory** (US 70). Steiger considered it glorified militarism; he was later to be offered roles George C. Scott had rejected.

☆ The role which won Claudette Colbert her Best Actress Oscar in **It Happened One Night** was turned down successively by **Myrna Loy**, **Margaret Sullavan**, **Miriam Hopkins** and **Constance Bennett**. Colbert only accepted it on condition that shooting was completed in four weeks and that her usual salary of $25,000 per picture was doubled to $50,000.

☆ Greer Garson was talked into playing **Mrs Miniver** (US 42) because **Norma Shearer** refused to play a mother role. Garson was equally reluctant but had less pull on the studio lot. Ironically her Oscar winning performance catapulted her to the top of the studio tree.

☆ When **Robert Donat** failed to turn up in Hollywood for **Captain Blood** (US 35), Warner Bros asked **Brian Aherne** to step into the lead, but he turned it down. Finally the studio took a chance and cast an unknown young Australian in the part–Errol Flynn.

☆ **Jeanne Moreau** was first choice for Mrs Robinson (Anne Bancroft) in **The Graduate** (US 67).

☆ **Audrey Hepburn** turned down the title role in **The Diary of Anne Frank** (US 59) in favour of the flop **Green Mansions** (US 59). As the only Dutch actress of international repute, she may have regretted passing up the opportunity to play the Dutch girl who has come to symbolise the tragedy of the holocaust.

☆ Deborah Kerr won her celebrated role in *From Here to Eternity* (US 53) because **Joan Crawford**, announced for the part, hated the costumes.

☆ **Princess Grace of Monaco** was originally scheduled to play Tippi Hedren's title role in Hitchcock's *Marnie* (US 64). Prince Rainier had agreed to her returning to the screen, but the Monagesques were shocked at the idea and it was dropped.

☆ Ginger Rogers replaced **Eleanor Parker** who replaced **Rita Hayworth** who replaced **Judy Garland** as Jean Harlow's mother in *Harlow* (US 65).

☆ **George Raft** gave the thumbs down to leading roles in *Dead End* (US 37), *High Sierra* (US 41), *The Maltese Falcon* (US 41) and *Casablanca* (US 42). They all went to Bogey.

☆ Michael Caine established his

Alfie *also known as Michael Caine.*

inimitable cockney persona in *Alfie* (GB 66) after the part had been turned down by **Anthony Newley**, **James Booth**, **Terence Stamp** and **Laurence Harvey**.

☆ Bogart was second choice for *The African Queen* (GB 51), as was Katherine Hepburn. The intention was to cast **David Niven** and **Bette Davis**.

☆ Perhaps a unique example of a starring role intended for an actor going instead to an actress was the lead in *The Spanish Dancer* (US 20). Written for **Rudolph Valentino**, it was rewritten for Pola Negri.

☆ **Rip Torn** was originally signed for the cameo role of the Texan lawyer in *Easy Rider* (US 69) that brought overnight celebrity to veteran supporting player Jack Nicholson.

☆ The *Road to ...* films were not designed for Bob Hope and Bing Crosby; they were meant for **Fred MacMurray** and **George Burns**.

☆ **Charles Laughton** began the part of Micawber in *David Copperfield* (US 35), but after three days of shooting became convinced that W. C. Fields was the only actor suitable for it. Paramount agreed to replace him, but with a condition written into Fields' contract that he had to speak in an English accent–an obligation he signally failed to fulfil!

☆ **George Segal** actually began filming *10* (US 79), but quit due to 'creative difficulties'–to be replaced by Dudley Moore in the role that shot the diminutive Englishman to Hollywood stardom.

☆ Original choice for James Bond

was none other than **Roger Moore**! Other contenders before Sean Connery was selected were **Patrick McGoohan**, **Trevor Howard**, **James Mason** and **Richard Burton**. Moore finally got to play 007 in the ninth Bond picture. As he declares that each Bondage is his last, speculation about his successor is rife. Can it really be true that James Coburn and Burt Reynolds are the two most favoured candidates to personify the suave English sophisticate?

☆ 1,400 actresses interviewed for the role of Scarlett O'Hara did not appear in *Gone With the Wind* (US 39), including the 400 who were given readings, the 60 who were screen tested, the three who expected to be chosen (**Joan Bennett**, **Jean Arthur** and **Paulette Goddard**) and the one (**Norma Shearer**) who claimed to have turned it down.

JUST BE YOURSELF

Most of the major stars have portrayed themselves in fictional films at one time or another. This is a brief selection of 20:

1 **Brigitte Bardot**
   in *Dear Brigitte* (US 65)
2 **Humphrey Bogart**
   in *The Love Lottery* (US 54)
3 **Charlie Chaplin**
   in *Show People* (US 29)
4 **Julie Christie**
   in *Nashville* (US 73)
5 **Gary Cooper**
   in *Starlift* (US 51)
6 **Marlene Dietrich**
   in *Jigsaw* (US 49)
7 **Henry Fonda**

   in *Feodora* (W. Ger 78)
8 **Greta Garbo**
   in *A Man's Man* (US 29)
10 **Cary Grant**
   in *Without Reservations* (US 46)
11 **Larry Hagman**
   in *I Am Blushing* (Swe 83)
12 **Liza Minnelli**
   in *Silent Movie* (US 76)
13 **Mary Pickford**
   in *The Kiss of Mary Pickford* (USSR 26)
14 **George Raft**
   in *Casino Royale* (GB 67)
15 **Ronald Reagan**
   in *It's a Great Feeling* (US 49)
16 **Martin Sheen**
   in *In the King of Prussia* (US 82)
17 **Frank Sinatra**
   in *Cannonball Run II* (US 83)
18 **Gloria Swanson**
   in *Airport 75* (US 74)
19 **Natalie Wood**
   in *The Candidate* (US 72)
20 **Susannah York**
   in *Long Shot* (GB 78)

FILM NAMES

Don't name your baby after a film star. Why not give it a film title instead?

Ada (US 61); *Adam* (Yug 77); *Adelaide* (Fr 68); *Adela* (Rum 85); *Adele* (US 19); *Adrien* (Fr 43); *Agatha* (GB 79) (S. Kor 85); *Alexandra* (Ger 14); *Alfie* (GB 66); *Alicia* (Neth 74); *Amy* (US 81); *Ana* (Por 82); *Andy* (US 65); *Angela* (US 55) (Neth/Bel 73) (Can 76) (Can 84); *Anna* (GB 18)

(USSR 36) (It 50) (Fr 52) (Fin 70) (Fr/Hun 81); **Angelina** (It 48); **Anne-Marie** (Fr 36); **Annie** (US 82); **Arabella** (Pol 17) (It 69); **Arnold** (US 73); **Arthur** (Fr 31) (US 81); **Audrey** (US 16); ☆ **Babette** (Fr 17); **Barbara** (US 70); **Barnaby** (GB 19); **Barney** (Aus 76); **Barry** (Fr 49); **Beatrice** (It 19); **Becky** (US 27); **Bedelia** (GB 46); **Belle** (Bel/Fr 73); **Ben** (US 72); **Benjamin** (Fr 68) (US 75); **Benji** (US 74); **Bernadine** (US 57); **Bertha** (US 27); **Betty** (Gre 82); **Bianca** (It 84); **Biddy** (GB 84); **Bill** (Fr 23); **Billie** (US 65); **Blanche** (Fr 71) ☆ **Camila** (Arg 84); **Carlota** (Hun 71); **Carrie** (US 52) (US 76); **Cathy** (SA 83); **Cecilia** (Fr/It 75) (Cuba 82); **Celeste** (Fr 70) (W. Ger 81); **Celia** (GB 49); **Charly** (US 68); **Charlotte** (W. Ger 81) (Neth 85); **Chloe** (GB 29); **Christa** (US/Den 71); **Christina** (US 29) (Arg 46) (W. Ger 50) (Can 74) (Sp 84); **Christine** (Fr 59) (US 83); **Clarence** (US 21) (US 37); **Clarissa** (Ger 41); **Claudia** (US 43); **Claudine** (Fr 40); **Constance** (NZ 84); **Cordelia** (Can 80); **Cynthia** (US 47) ☆ **Dan** (US 14); **Daniel** (US 83); **Daphne** (Jap 66); **David** (GB 51) (US 79); **Davy** (GB 57); **Dawn** (Aus 77); **Diana** (Ger 29); **Diane** (US 55); **Dino** (US 57); **Dolly** (Fr 28); **Dolores** (Sp 49); **Dominique** (GB 79); **Donatella** (It 56); **Dora** (GB 27); **Douglas** (Nor 70); **Dulcima** (GB 71); **Dulcy** (US 23) (US 40) ☆ **Elisa** (Fr 57); **Elise** (Den 85); **Ellie** (US 84); **Elsa, Elsa!** (Fr 85); **Emily** (GB 77); **Emma** (US 32) (GB 65); **Emma Mae** (US 76); **Emmanuelle** (Fr 74); **Esmeralda** (US 15) (GB 22); **Esther** (GB 16); **Eva** (Austria 35) (Fr/It 62) (Yug 85); **Evangeline** (Can 14) (US 19) ☆ **Fanny** (Fr 32) (Fr 48) (US 61); **Felicite** (Fr 79); **Felicity** (Aus 77); **Felix** (Den 82); **Fran** (Aus 85); **Frances** (US 82); **Francis** (US 49); **Francisca** (Port 81); **Franz** (Fr/Bel 72); **Frederica** (Ger 33); **Frieda** (US 47) ☆ **Gabriela** (W. Ger 50) (Br 83); **Gabriella** (US 85); **Gaby** (US 56); **Genevieve** (GB 53); **George** (US 73); **Georgia, Georgia** (US 77); **Geraldine** (US 29) (Fr 53); **Gertrud** (Den 64); **Gigi** (Fr 49) (US 58); **Gilda** (US 46); **Gloria** (Fr 77) (US 80); **Gus** (US 76); **Gwen** (Fr 85) ☆ **Harvey** (US 50); **Hector** (Sp 84); **Hedda** (GB 77); **Helena** (Ger 24); **Helene** (Fr 36) ☆ **Inga** (Swe 68); **Isabel** (Can 68); **Isadora** (GB 68); **Irene** (US 26) (US 40); **Iris** (GB 15) (Israel 68) (NZ 84); **Ivy** (US 47) ☆ **Jack** (Fr 14) (Swe 77); **Jacqueline** (GB 56) (W. Ger 59); **Janie** (US 44); **Jasmine** (GB 12); **Jassy** (GB 47); **Jeannie** (GB 40); **Jeff** (Fr/It 69); **Jennie** (US 41); **Jennifer** (US 78); **Jenny** (Pol 36) (Neth/W. Ger 58) (US 69); **Jeremy** (US 73); **Jessica** (US 62); **Jimmy** (GB 16); **Jo** (Fr 71); **Joan** (Fr 85); **Joanna** (US 25) (GB 68); **Jocelyn** (Fr 22) (Fr 52); **Joe** (US 70); **Joey** (W. Ger 85); **Jonas** (W. Ger 57); **Jonathan** (W. Ger 73); **Joni** (US 80); **Josette** (US 38); **Joshua** (US 76); **Joy** (US 77) (Fr/Can 84); **Judith** (US 65); **Judy** (Aus 71); **Julia** (W. Ger 75) (US 77); **Julie** (US 56); **Julietta** (Fr 53); **Justine** (US 69) ☆ **Kate** (US 14); **Kathleen** (GB 37) (US 41); **Katrina** (Swe 49); **Kelly** (Can 81); **Kitty** (GB 29) (US 45) ☆ **Laura** (US 44) (W. Ger 63); **Lenny** (US 74); **Leonara** (Aus 86); **Lianna** (US 82); **Lila** (W. Ger/Swe 62); **Lili** (US 53); **Lilli Marlene** (GB 50); **Lily Christine** (GB 32); **Linda** (US 29) (GB 60) (W. Ger/Sp 81); **Lisa** (US 63); **Lizzie** (US 57) (NZ 84); **Lola** (US 14) (Fr 61) (W. Ger 81); **Lolita** (GB 62); **Lorna** (Can 64); **Louie** (Thai 77); **Louise** (Fr 39) (Fr 85); **Lucia** (Cuba 68);

29

Lucie (Nor 79); *Lucy* (W. Ger 85); *Lulu* (Ger 28) (Austria 62) (US 78) (Fr/W. Ger/It 80); *Lydia* (US 41) (Can 64) (W. Ger 70)

☆ *Madeleine* (GB 50); *Magda* (US 17); *Maisie* (US 39); *Maisie Lou* (GB 29); *Malcolm* (Aus 85); *Mandy* (GB 52); *Manuela* (GB 57); *Marcella* (It 37); *Margie* (US 40) (US 16); *Maria* (Swe 47) (Swe 75) (Port 79) (Neth 85); *Marian* (Sp 79); *Marianne* (US 29) (US 77); *Marie* (Ger 33) (W. Ger 72) (US 85); *Marie-Ann* (Can 78); *Marie-Claire* (Aus 85); *Marie-Louise* (Swz 45); *Marigold* (GB 38); *Marilyn* (GB 53) (US 63); *Mario* (It 84); *Marlene* (W. Ger 84); *Marnie* (US 64); *Marta* (It/Sp 71); *Martha* (GB 22) (GB 27) (W. Ger 74); *Martin* (US 78); *Marty* (US 55); *Mary* (GB 09) (Ger 31); *Maryjane* (US 68); *Mary Lou* (US 48); *Matilda* (US 78); *Matt* (GB 18); *Maud* (GB 11); *Meg* (GB 26); *Melanie* (Can 82); *Melinda* (US 72); *Melody* (GB 71); *Michael* (Ger 24) (US 48); *Mickey* (US 18) (US 48); *Mike* (US 25); *Millie* (US 31); *Mimi* (GB 35); *Minnie* (US 23); *Mira* (Neth/Bel 71); *Miranda* (GB 48) (It 85); *Molly* (Aus 83); *Mona* (US 71); *Monica* (NZ 86); *Monique* (GB 70) (Fr/US 85); *Myriam* (Gre) 82 ☆ *Nadia* (US 84); *Nance* (GB 20); *Nancy* (GB 22); *Nana* (Swe 71); *Natalia* (Chile 70); *Nathalie* (Fr/It 57) (Gre 80); *Nell* (GB 29); *Nelly* (GB 15) ☆ *Octavia* (US 82); *Odette* (Fr 28) (GB 50); *Oliver!* (GB 68); *Olivia* (Fr 51) (Fr/Bel 85); *Oscar* (Fr 67) ☆ *Paddy* (Eire 70); *Patrick* (Aus 78); *Patsy* (US 23); *Patty* (US 76); *Paul* (Fr 67); *Paula* (GB 15) (US 52); *Paulette* (Fr 86); *Peggy* (US 16) (US 50); *Penelope* (US 66); *Percy* (GB 71); *Peter* (Hun 35); *Petulia* (GB 68); *Polly* (GB 21); *Poppy* (US 17) (US 36); *Polly Ann* (US 17); *Prunella*

(US 18) ☆ *Queenie* (US 21) ☆ *Rachel. Rachel* (US 68); *Raymond* (Fr 38); *Rebecca* (US 40); *Richard* (US 72); *Rita* (Fr 50) (Latvia 58) (Por 82); *Roberta* (US 35); *Ronnie* (US 73); *Ronny* (Ger 32); *Rosa* (Gre 82); *Rosalie* (US 37); *Rose* (Fr 36); *Rosemarie* (W. Ger 58); *Rose Marie* (US 28) (US 36) (US 54); *Rosemary* (US 15); *Rosie* (US 67); *Ruby* (US 77); *Rufus* (Neth 75) ☆ *Sabrina* (US 55); *Sally* (US 29); *Sandra* (US 24); *Sandy* (US 18) (US 26); *Sarah* (Aus 81) (Fr 83); *Sebastian* (GB 67) (US 76); *Sebastiane* (GB 76); *Serena* (GB 62); *Shamus* (GB 59); *Sheena* (US 84); *Shirley* (GB 22); *Simon* (US 80); *Simon, Simon* (GB 70); *Sonia* (GB 21); *Sophia* (Pol 77); *Stanley* (Aus 84); *Stella* (GB 21) (Arg 43) (US 50) (Gre 55) (Fr 83); *Stevie* (GB 78); *Susana* (Mex 51); *Suzanna* (US 23); *Suzanne* (Can 80) (Fr 83); *Suzy* (US 36); *Sybil* (GB 21); *Sylvia* (US 65) (NZ 85) ☆ *Tansy* (GB 21); *Tanya* (USSR 42); *Teresa* (US 51) (Fr 70); *Tesha* (GB 28); *Tess* (GB/Fr 81); *Thelma* (GB 18) (US 22); *Theodora* (It 21); *Thomas* (Fr 75); *Tillie* (US 22); *Tim* (Aus 79); *Tish* (US 42); *Tom* (US 73); *Tommy* (Hun 37) (GB 75); *Toni* (GB 28) (Fr 35) ☆ *Una* (Yug 85) ☆ *Valerie* (Can 69); *Vanessa* (W. Ger 77); *Veronica* (Ger 27); *Véronique* (Fr 49); *Vicki* (Fr 53); *Victor* (Fr 51); *Victoria* (Ger 35) (Swe/W. Ger 79); *Viki* (Hun 37); *Violet* (Yug 78); *Viviette* (US 18) ☆ *Wally* (It 32); *Wanda* (US 70); *Willie* (US 81); *Willy* (W. Ger 63); *Wilma* (US 77) ☆ *Yolande* (Mex 43); *Yvette* (Ger 38); *Yvonne* (GB 15) ☆ *Zachariah* (US 70); *Zaza* (US 15) (US 28); *Zoe* (Fr 54); *Zoya* (USSR 45).

RELATIVELY SPEAKING

□□□□□□□□□□□□□□□□□□□

STARS RELATED TO OTHER STARS

This list is confined to related stars who perform under different surnames.

☆ **Katherine Houghton** is the niece of **Katherine Hepburn**–played her daughter in *Guess Who's Coming to Dinner* (US 67)

☆ **Sally Blane** is the sister of **Loretta Young**.

☆ **Dana Andrews** is the brother of **Steve Forrest** (both born in small Mississippi town with the odd name of Don't).

☆ **Scott Brady** is the brother of **Lawrence Tierney**.

☆ **Robert Morley** was the son-in-law of **Gladys Cooper**.

☆ **Sally Field** is the step-daughter of **Jock 'Tarzan' Mahoney**.

☆ **Viola Dana**, **Edna Fulgarth** and **Shirley Mason** were sisters.

☆ **Jamie Lee Curtis** is the daughter of **Janet Leigh** and **Tony Curtis**.

☆ **Larry Hagman** is the son of **Mary Martin**.

☆ **Pier Angeli** and **Marisa Pavan** are twin sisters.

☆ **Maria Schneider** is the illegitimate daughter of **Daniel Gélin** (a fact of which she was unaware until she was 16).

☆ **Rip Torn** is the cousin of **Sissy Spacek**.

☆ **Joely Richardson** is the daughter of **Vanessa Redgrave** (and the granddaughter of **Sir Michael Redgrave** and **Rachel Kempson** and the great granddaughter of Australian silent screen star **Roy Redgrave**).

☆ **Al 'Fuzzy' St John** was the cousin of **Roscoe 'Fatty' Arbuckle**.

☆ **Dolores del Rio** was the second cousin of **Ramon Novarro**.

☆ **James MacArthur** is the son of **Helen Hayes**.

☆ **Rita Hayworth** is the first cousin of **Ginger Rogers** (their

Lela and Ginger Rogers, aunt and first cousin of Rita Hayworth (right).

Mother: Maureen O'Sullivan.

Daughter: Mia Farrow.

mothers were sisters).

☆ **Tom Conway** was the brother of **George Sanders**.

☆ **Carrie Fisher** is the daughter of **Debbie Reynolds**.

☆ **Françoise Dorleac** was the sister of **Catherine Deneueve**.

☆ **Mia Farrow** is the daughter of **Maureen O'Sullivan**

☆ **Liza Minnelli** is the daughter of **Judy Garland**.

☆ **Kay Hammond** was the daughter of 'Hollywood's most aristocratic actor' **Sir Guy Standing**.

☆ **Janette Scott** is the daughter of **Thora Hird**.

☆ Brat Pack youth hero **Emilio Esterez** of *The Breakfast Club* and *St Elmo's Fire* is the son of **Martin Sheen**.

STARS RELATED TO OTHER NOTABLE PEOPLE

☆ **Lex 'Tarzan' Barker** is descended from Roger Williams, who founded the colony of Rhode

Island in 1636.

☆ **Wendy Barrie** was the granddaughter of Sir Charles Warren, head of Scotland Yard (and goddaughter of J. M. Barrie).

☆ **Anne Baxter** was the granddaughter of Frank Lloyd Wright.

☆ **Jean-Paul Belmondo** is the son of the celebrated French sculptor Paul Belmondo.

☆ **Marisa Berenson** is the grand-niece of art historian Bernard Berenson and the granddaughter of couturier Elsa Schiaparelli.

☆ **Hobart Bosworth** was descended from Myles Standish, military leader aboard the *Mayflower*.

☆ **Helena Bonham-Carter**, newly-minted star of *A Room with a View* (GB 86) and *Lady Jane* (GB 86), is the great-niece of director Anthony Asquith and great-great-niece of Prime Minister Herbert Asquith.

☆ **Donald Calthrop** was the nephew of Irish dramatist Dion Boucicault (whose *The Colleen Bawn* was filmed several times).

☆ **Leo Carillo** was the great-grandson of Carlos Antonio Carillo, Governor of the then Mexican province of California in 1837.

☆ **Geraldine Chaplin** is the granddaughter of playwright Eugene O'Neill.

☆ **Montgomery Clift** was the great-grandson of Major Robert Anderson, Commander of Fort Sumter at the outbreak of the American Civil War.

☆ **Ivy Close**, Edwardian beauty queen who became star of early silents, was the mother of director Ronald Neame.

☆ **Wendell Corey** was descended from John Quincy Adams, 6th US President, and John Adams, 2nd US President.

☆ **Melvyn Douglas** was the son of concert pianist Edouard Hesselberg.

☆ **Marie Dressler** was the daughter of Alexander von Koerber, the last surviving British officer of the Crimean War (enlisted after deserting from Prussian army and was promoted from ranks).

☆ **Nelson Eddy** was descended from Martin Van Buren, US President 1837–41 (see also Glenn Ford).

☆ **Faye Emerson** was the daughter-in-law of President Franklin D. Roosevelt (married his son Elliott in 1944).

☆ **Geraldine Fitzgerald** is a distant cousin of James Joyce. (He mentions the family firm, D & T Fitzgerald of Dublin, in *Ulysses*. Joyce was also in the movie business–he was manager of the first cinema in Ireland.)

☆ **Errol Flynn** was a distant cousin of Princess Diana.

☆ **Glenn Ford** was the nephew of Sir John MacDonald, 1st Prime Minister of Canada in 1867, and was descended from Martin Van Buren, US President 1837–41 (see also Nelson Eddy).

☆ **Judy Garland** was a collateral of General Ulysses S. Grant, US President 1869–77–her great-grandfather, Hugh Fitzpatrick, was his first cousin.

☆ **Richard Greene** is the grandson of British pioneer of cinematography William Friese-Greene–subject of biopic *The Magic Box* (GB 51).

☆ **Joyce Grenfell** was the niece of Nancy Astor.

☆ **Nigel Havers** is the son of Attorney-General Sir Michael Havers.

☆ **June Havoc** was the sister of pioneer striptease artiste Gypsy Rose Lee–subject of biopic *Gypsy* (US 62).

☆ **Margaux** and **Mariel Hemingway** are the granddaughters of Ernest Hemingway.

☆ **William Holden**'s mother was the second cousin of Warren G. Harding, US President 1921–23.

☆ **Boris Karloff** was the brother of distinguished diplomat Sir John Pratt.

☆ **Elissa Landi** was the granddaughter of the Empress Elizabeth of Austria (her mother was the Empress's illegitimate daughter).

☆ **Angela Lansbury** is the granddaughter of George Lansbury, Leader of the Labour Party 1931–35 and founder of the *Daily Herald*.

☆ **Peter Lawford** was brother-in-law of President John F. Kennedy (married to his sister Patricia).

*Sisters Margaux and Mariel Hemingway played the two sisters in **Lipstick***.

☆ **Sophia Loren** is the sister of Mussolini's daughter-in-law.

☆ **John Mills** is the brother of pioneer TV personality Annette Mills of Muffin the Mule fame.

☆ **Marilyn Monroe** claimed to be descended from James Monroe, US President 1817–25, through her maternal grandmother Della Hogan Monroe Grainger.

☆ **James Pierce**, one of the pre-Weissmuller Tarzans, was son-in-law of Tarzan's creator Edgar Rice Burroughs.

☆ **Christopher Plummer** is the great-grandson of Sir John Abbott, Prime Minister of Canada 1891–2.

☆ **Jane Powell** is the daughter-in-law of former lightweight boxing champion of the world Willie Ritchie.

☆ **Vincent Price** is descended from Peregrine White, first caucasian child born in Massachusetts (1620).

☆ **Basil Rathbone** was descended from King Henry IV (reigned 1399–1413) on his mother's side.

☆ **Oliver Reed** is the nephew of director Sir Carol Reed.

☆ **Anne Revere**, who won Best Supporting Actress Oscar for ***National Velvet*** (US 44), is descended from Paul Revere.

☆ **Cesar Romero** is the grandson of Jose Marti, liberator of Cuba.

☆ **Arnold Schwarzenneger** is the son-in-law of President Kennedy's sister Eunice.

☆ **Martha Scott**'s mother was first cousin of William McKinley, US President 1897–1901.

☆ **Charles Stevens**, diminutive Apache who played 'pesky injuns' from ***The Birth of a Nation*** (US 15) to ***The Outsider*** (US 61), was the grandson of Geronimo.

☆ **Nora Swinburne** is descended from Algernon Charles Swinburne, poet.

☆ **Jon Voigt** is the brother of singer-songwriter Chip Taylor.

☆ **Jane Wyatt** is descended from Philip Livingstone, signatory of the Declaration of Independence.

KEEPING IT IN THE FAMILY

Relatives who have played the same relationship on screen:

☆ **Richard** and **Constance Bennett** as father and daughter in *Bought* (US 31)

☆ **Francine** and **Colette Bergé** as sisters in *Les Abysses* (Fr 63)

☆ **James Cagney** and **Jeanne Cagney** as brother and sister in *Yankee Doodle Dandy* (US 42)

☆ **David**, **Keith** and **Robert Carradine** as the Younger brothers; **James** and **Stacy Keach** as Jesse and Frank James; **Dennis** and **Randy Quaid** as the Miller boys; **Christopher** and **Nicholas Guest** as the Ford brothers in *The Long Riders* (US 80)

☆ **Diane Cilento** and **Jason Connery** as mother and son in *The Boy Who Had Everything* (Aus 85)

☆ **Catherine Deneuve** and **Françoise Dorleac** as sisters in *Les Portes Claquent* (Fr 60); *Ce Soir ou Jamais* (Fr 60); *La Chasse a l'Homme* (Fr 64); *Les Demoiselles de Rochefort* (Fr 67)

☆ **Lillian** and **Dorothy Gish** as sisters in *Orphans of the Storm* (US 21)

☆ **Margaux** and **Mariel Hemingway** as sisters in *Lipstick* (US 76)

☆ **Mervyn** and **Glynis Johns** as father and daughter in *The Halfway House* (GB 43)

☆ **Joe** and **Buster Keaton** as father and son in *Neighbors* (US 20)

☆ **Geoffrey Kendal**, **Laura Liddel** (Mrs Kendal) and **Felicity Kendal** as father, mother and daughter in *Shakespeare*

*Buster Keaton was famous for not smiling. His real-life father Joe Keaton, who played Buster's father in **Neighbors**, looked pretty doleful too.*

Sir Michael Redgrave and daughter Vanessa played father and daughter in **Behind the Mask**.

Wallah (India 65)

☆ **Alan Ladd** and **David Ladd** as father and son in *The Proud Rebel* (US 58)

☆ **Raymond** and **Daniel Massey** as father and son in *The Queen's Guards* (GB 61)

☆ **John** and **Hayley Mills** as father and daughter in *The Truth About Spring* (GB 65)

☆ **John** and **Juliet Mills** as father and daughter in *In Which We Serve* (GB 42) and *The History of Mr Polly* (GB 49)

☆ **Ryan O'Neal** and **Tatum O'Neal** as probably father and daughter in *Paper Moon* (US 73) – it is never revealed whether he is her father

☆ **Priscilla Pointer** and **Amy Irving** as mother and daughter in *Carrie* (US 76)

☆ **Anthony** and **Duncan Quinn** as father and son in *The Children of Sanchez* (US 78) and *Caravans* (US 78)

☆ **Sir Michael** and **Vanessa Redgrave** as father and daughter in *Behind the Mask* (GB 58)

☆ **Ginger** and **Lela Rogers** as mother and daughter in *The Major and the Minor* (US 42)

☆ **George Sanders** and **Tom Conway** as the Falcon and his brother in *The Falcon's Brother* (US 42)

☆ **Magda** and **Romy Schneider** as mother and daughter in *Wenn der Weisse Flieder Wieder Blüht* (W. Ger 53)

☆ **Mario** and **Megan Van Peebles** as brother and sister in *South Bronx Heroes* (US 85)

☆ **Googie Withers** and **Joanna McCallum** as mother and daughter in *Nickel Queen* (Aus 71)

☆ **Loretta Young, Sally Blane, Polly Ann Young** and **Georgianna Young** as sisters in *The Story of Alexander Graham Bell* (US 39)

TOP NOTCH

KNIGHTS OF THE SILVER SCREEN

The following film actors have been knighted for their services to the theatre and/or screen:

Sir Cedric Hardwicke 1934
Sir C. Aubrey Smith 1944
Sir Ralph Richardson 1947
Sir Laurence Olivier 1947
(Lord Olivier 1970)
Sir John Gielgud 1953
Sir Donald Wolfit 1957
Sir Alec Guinness 1959
Sir Michael Redgrave 1959
Sir Felix Aylmer 1965
Sir John Clements 1968
Sir Robert Helpmann 1968
Sir Bernard Miles 1969
(Lord Miles 1979)
Sir Noel Coward 1970
Sir Charles Chaplin 1975
Sir Stanley Baker 1976
Sir Richard Attenborough 1976
Sir John Mills 1976
Sir Michael Hordern 1983
Sir Anthony Quayle 1986

Sir Guy Standing, described in the 1930s as 'the most aristocratic actor in Hollywood', was knighted in 1919 in recognition of a British war mission to the USA. Douglas Fairbanks Jr was knighted in 1949 for promoting Anglo-US relations. As an American citizen he accepted the accolade without adopting the title. Sir C. Aubrey Smith was knighted in 1944 as 'a leading member of the British community in California', though as this meant in effect the expatriate film community in Hollywood, he is included in the list above.

Film actresses created DBE for services to theatre and/or screen:

Dame Sybil Thorndike 1931
Dame Irene Vanbrugh 1941
Dame Edith Evans 1946
Dame Peggy Ashcroft 1954
Dame Judith Anderson 1960
Dame Flora Robson 1960
Dame Gladys Cooper 1967
Dame Margaret Rutherford 1967
Dame Anna Neagle 1967
Dame Wendy Hiller 1975
Dame Gracie Fields 1979
Dame Celia Johnson 1981

Dame May Whitty's DBE was conferred on her in 1918 for war services.

The film involving the services of the most theatrical knights, existing or prospective, was *Oh, What a Lovely War* (GB 69). The cast included the following:

Sir John Clements
(General Von Molke)
Sir Ralph Richardson
(Sir Edward Grey)
Sir Michael Redgrave
(General Sir Henry Wilson)
Sir John Gielgud
(Count Berchtold)
Sir Laurence Olivier
(Field Marshal Sir John French)
Sir John Mills
(Field Marshal Sir Douglas Haig)
Director: (Sir) Richard Attenborough

Finally a word from Australia's Dame Judith Anderson on what the cherished accolade meant to her: 'Having been made a Dame has made a slight difference to my life. I find myself wearing gloves more often.'

□□□□□□□□□□□□□□□□□□□□□□□

OLIVIER

Acknowledged by many as the greatest living actor, Sir Laurence Olivier is arguably also the most versatile. Certainly few major stars have played so many literary or historical characters, nor so many different nationalities, as this selection of his movie roles will testify.

Eighteenth-century Italian balloonist Vincent Lunardi in *Conquest of the Air* (GB 35)

Russian officer in *Moscow Nights* (GB 35)

Orlando in *As You Like It* (GB 36)

Elizabethan soldier-spy in *Fire Over England* (GB 37)

Heathcliff in *Wuthering Heights* (US 39)

Mr Darcy in *Pride and Prejudice* (US 40)

Maxim de Winter in *Rebecca* (US 40)

French-Canadian fur trapper in *49th Parallel* (GB 41)

Nelson in *That Hamilton Woman* (US 42)

Russian engineer in *The Demi-Paradise* (GB 43)

Henry V in *Henry V* (GB 44)

Hamlet in *Hamlet* (GB 48)

Cockney policeman in *The Magic Box* (GB 51)

Chicago restaurant manager in *Carrie* (US 52)

Macheath in *The Beggar's Opera* (GB 53)

Richard III in *Richard III* (GB 55)

Ruritanian prince in *The Prince and the Showgirl* (GB 57)

General Burgoyne in *The Devil's Disciple* (GB 59)

Has-been music hall comic Archie Rice in *The Entertainer* (GB 60)

Roman senator in *Spartacus* (US 61)

Schoolmaster accused of raping pupil in *Term of Trial* (GB 62)

Scotland Yard Inspector in *Bunny Lake Is Missing* (GB 62)

Othello in *Othello* (GB 65)

The Mahdi, Sudanese religious zealot, in *Khartoum* (GB 66)

Soviet premier in *The Shoes of the Fisherman* (US 68)

Swedish army officer in Strindberg's *The Dance of Death* (GB 69)

Field Marshal Sir John French in *Oh, What a Lovely War* (GB 69)

Lord Dowding in *The Battle of Britain* (GB 69)

Mr Creakle in *David Copperfield* (GB 70)

Russian doctor in Chekhov's *The Three Sisters* (GB 70)

Count Witte, Russian premier, in *Nicholas and Alexandra* (GB 71)

Duke of Wellington in *Lady Caroline Lamb* (GB 72)

Homicidal writer in *Sleuth* (GB 72)

Nazi dentist in *The Marathon Man* (US 76)

Professor Moriarty in *The Seven Per Cent Solution* (GB 76)

Dutch doctor in *A Bridge Too Far* (GB 77)

Nicodemus in *Jesus of Nazareth* (GB/It 77)

American auto manufacturing tycoon in *The Betsy* (US 78)

Van Hesling in *Dracula* (US 79)

French boulevardier in *A Little Romance* (US/Fr 79)–his 60th film role

Jewish Nazi hunter from Mittel Europa in *The Boys from Brazil* (US 78)

Jewish cantor in *The Jazz Singer* (US 80)

Zeus in *Clash of the Titans* (GB 81)

General McArthur in *Inchon* (S. Korea/US 81)

Bavarian courtier in *Wagner* (GB 83)

Rudolf Hess in *Wild Geese II* (GB 85)

THE THREE MOST ENDURING STARS

Every year since 1931, Quigley Publications have polled US exhibitors to ascertain which stars have drawn the biggest audiences. The three names appearing most often in the annual list of Top Ten Money-Making Stars are as follows:

1	**John Wayne**	25 listings
=2	**Gary Cooper**	18 listings
=2	**Clint Eastwood**	18 listings*

* To 1985 inclusive

KING VIDOR'S THREE BEST ACTRESSES

King Vidor, whose career as a director was the longest ever (66 years), directed more actresses than most. These, in his opinion, were the three best performances:

1 **Laurette Taylor** as Peg in *Peg O' My Heart* (US 23)

2 **Lillian Gish** as Mimi in *La Bohème* (US 26)

3 **Audrey Hepburn** as Natasha in *War and Peace* (US 56)

RADIO CITY MUSIC HALL'S ALL-TIME GREATS

Radio City Music Hall was said to have first pick of all the best movies playing New York. The three biggest drawing stars, in terms of the number of their movies show-cased at the Music Hall with the cumulative run, were:

1	**Cary Grant**	28 movies 113 weeks
2	**Katherine Hepburn**	22 movies 64 weeks
3	**Fred Astaire**	16 movies 60 weeks

ROBERT DONAT'S FIVE GREATEST SCREEN PERFORMERS

☆ **Charles Chaplin**

☆ **Deanna Durbin**

☆ **Greta Garbo**

☆ **Paul Muni**

☆ **Spencer Tracy**

Muni returned the compliment by declaring Donat 'the greatest actor we have today'.

EASTMAN HOUSE TEN GREATEST PERFORMERS

In 1952 Eastman House sponsored a Festival of the Arts at which they honoured the ten performers who had contributed most to the art of the movies. In alphabetical order:

☆ **Richard Barthelmess**
☆ **Charles Chaplin**
☆ **Ronald Colman**
☆ **Lillian Gish**
☆ **Buster Keaton**
☆ **Harold Lloyd**
☆ **Mae Marsh**
☆ **Mary Pickford**
☆ **Gloria Swanson**
☆ **Norma Talmadge**

OSCAR ODDITIES

The main records relating to the Academy Awards–most wins, most nominations, oldest and youngest winners, co-stars who have won, etc–are contained in *The Guinness Book of Film Facts & Feats*. This list notes some of the lesser known facts about Hollywood's most prestigious award.

☆ The only tie for Best Actor was in 1932, when Wallace Beery, honoured for *The Champ*, split his Oscar with Fredric March, honoured for *Dr Jekyll and Mr Hyde*.

☆ The only tie for Best Actress was between Barbra Streisand, honoured for *Funny Girl* (US 68), and Katherine Hepburn, honoured for *The Lion in Winter* (GB 68).

☆ The first British film honoured with an award was *The Private Life of Henry VIII* (GB 34), for which Charles Laughton was awarded Best Actor. The first to win Best Film was *Hamlet* (GB 48).

☆ The first British actor to win an award was George Arliss with Best

Actor for *Disraeli* (US 29). First British actress to win was Vivien Leigh with Best Actress for *Gone With the Wind* (US 39).

☆ When Spencer Tracy won his first Oscar for *Captains Courageous* (US 37), the statuette was found to be inscribed, much to the Academy's embarrassment, 'To Dick Tracy'.

☆ The only occasion when three out of four Best Actor nominations were for stars in the same film was in 1935, with Clark Gable, Charles Laughton and Franchot Tone nominated for their performances in *Mutiny on the Bounty*. The winner was the fourth nominee, Victor McLaglen, for *The Informer*.

☆ Shelley Winters' Best Supporting Actress award for *The Diary of Anne Frank* (US 50) was presented to her at the house in Amsterdam where Anne Frank hid for 25 months before her capture and tragic death.

☆ The first posthumous Oscar was awarded to Sidney Howard for the screenplay of *Gone With the Wind* (US 39). He had been killed in a farm accident.

☆ Two film stars have won the Grand Slam of Oscar, Emmy, Tony and Grammy awards; Rita Moreno and Liza Minnelli.

☆ The most Oscars won at a single presentation were four by Walt Disney in 1953: Best Cartoon (*Toot, Whistle, Plunk and Boom*); Best Documentary Short (*The Alaskan Eskimo*); Best Documentary Feature (*The Living Desert*); Best Two-Reel Short (*Bear Country*).

☆ John Mills accepted the Oscar he won for playing a deaf mute in

Ryan's Daughter (GB 70) without speaking. Louise Fletcher's sign language when she won the Best Actress award for *One Flew Over the Cuckoo's Nest* (US 75) was addressed to her parents. They were both deaf.

☆ Two years before declining his Oscar for *The Godfather* (US 71), Marlon Brando had applied to the Academy for a replacement of the Oscar he had won for *On the Waterfront* (US 54), which had been stolen.

☆ From 1929 through 1985 a total of 277 men were nominated for Best Director and one woman. The sole femme helmer was Lina Wertmuller for *Seven Beauties* in 1976.

☆ The first telecast of the awards ceremony was made by NBC from the RKO Pantages Theatre, Hollywood, on 19 March 1953. The first in colour was made by ABC from Santa Monica Civic Auditorium on 18 April 1966.

☆ No Californian performer won an Oscar until 1963, when Gregory Peck took Best Actor for *To Kill a Mockingbird*. His fellow citizens of the small town of La Jolla, California, may have expected to wait a considerable time before such an honour befell another native son. In fact they only had to wait five years–Cliff Robertson, born at La Jolla in 1925, won Best Actor for *Charly* (US 68).

☆ The first person to refuse an Oscar was Dudley Nichols, screenwriter of *The Informer* (US 35). The reason was a union boycott of the awards ceremony that year.

☆ The only time an Oscar winner has been disqualified after receiving the award was in 1968,

Richard Burton scored his fifth Oscar nomination for *Anne of the Thousand Days*, but he never won an Oscar.

when Best Documentary *The Young Americans* was nixed after it was revealed that it had been shown theatrically the preceding calendar year. The Oscar was recalled.

☆ A dozen stars who never won an Oscar for an individual screen performance: Warren Beatty; Richard Burton; Montgomery Clift; Marlene Dietrich; Greta Garbo; Judy Garland; Cary Grant; Deborah Kerr; Myrna Loy; Marilyn Monroe; Paul Newman; Robert Redford.

☆ Only two non-professionals have won acting Oscars: Canadian war veteran Harold Russell for his role as the handless ex-soldier (Russell himself had had his hands blown off) in *The Best Years of Our Lives* (US 46); and Cambodian refugee Dr Haing S. Ngor for his moving performance as a victim of Cambodia's Pol Pot regime in *The Killing Fields* (GB 84).

☆ The most nominated films to receive no awards were *The Turning Point* (US 77), and *The*

The Color Purple (US 86), each with 11 nominations.

☆ The most nominated star never to have won an Oscar was Richard Burton, with six nominations: *My Cousin Rachel* (US 52); *The Robe* (US 53); *The Spy Who Came In From the Cold* (GB 65); *Who's Afraid of Virginia Woolf* (US 66); *Anne of the Thousand Days* (GB 70); *Equus* (GB 77). Geraldine Page won hers at the eighth attempt for *The Trip to Bountiful* in 1986.

☆ The reason Woody Allen was unable to pick up his three Oscars for *Annie Hall* (US 77)–Best Picture, Best Director, Best Screenwriter–was that he had a regular Monday night engagement playing clarinet at a Manhattan jazz cellar and he did not want to let down the boys.

☆ The only family to have contained three generations of Oscar winners is the Hustons. Walter Huston won Best Supporting Actor in 1948 for *The Treasure of the Sierra Madre*, his son John won Best Director for the same film, and John's daughter Anjelika won Best Supporting Actress for *Prizzi's Honour* in 1986.

☆ The Oscar ceremony is televised to 85 countries, including Red China. France, perhaps the most cinematic country in the world, resisted until 1986, then caved in to the lure of Hollywood, the most cinematic town in the world.

☆ The first person to know the identity of the Oscar winners is the anonymous auditor at accountancy firm Price Waterhouse & Co whose job it is to count the votes from the 4,200 voting members of the Academy of Motion Picture Arts and Sciences.

MONEY MATTERS

IT PAYS WELL . . .

A review of the top salary earners of each decade.

☆ *1910s*

Florence Lawrence $250 pw 1912

Asta Nielsen $1,500 pw (Germany) 1912

Mary Pickford $500 pw 1913

Mary Pickford $1,000 pw 1914

Mary Pickford $4,000 pw 1914

Francesca Bertini $3,365 pw (Italy) 1915

Charles Chaplin $12,884 pw 1916

Mary Pickford $10,000 pw plus bonuses 1916

Roscoe Arbuckle $1 million pa guaranteed minimum 1919

☆ *1920s*

Nazimova $13,000 pw 1920

Jackie Coogan $22,500 pw (of

which he was allowed $6.50–his mother spent the rest) 1924

Rudolph Valentino $10,000 pw plus % 1925

Tom Mix $17,500 pw 1925

Harold Lloyd $40,000 pw 1926

John Gilbert $10,000 pw 1928

Al Jolson $500,000 per film 1929

☆ *1930s*

Constance Bennett $30,000 pw 1931

John Barrymore $30,000 pw 1931

Greta Garbo $250,000 each for *The Painted Veil* (US 34) and *Anna Karenina* (US 35)

Mae West $480,833 pa 1935

Carole Lombard $465,000 pa 1937

Shirley Temple $307,014 pa 1938

Claudette Colbert $426,944 pa 1938

James Cagney $368,333 pa 1939

☆ *1940s*

Jeanette MacDonald $300,000 1941

Charles Boyer $350,000 1941

Bing Crosby $336,000 pa 1942

Betty Grable $800,000 pa 1945

Bette Davis $365,000 pa 1948

John Wayne $750,000 (on %) for *The Wake of the Red Witch* (US 48)

☆ *1950s*

Cary Grant $300,000 for *People Will Talk* (US 51)

James Stewart over $1 million (on %) for *The Glenn Miller Story* (US 54)

Gregory Peck $350,000 each for *The Million Pound Note* (GB 54)

and *The Purple Plain* (GB 54)

Elizabeth Taylor $500,000 each for *Cat On a Hot Tin Roof* (US 58) and *Suddenly Last Summer* (GB 59)

William Holden $750,000 plus 20% of net profits for *The Horse Soldiers* (US 59)

John Wayne ditto

☆ *1960s*

Cary Grant $3 million (on %) for *Operation Petticoat* (US 60) and the same for *That Touch of Mink* (US 62)

Clark Gable $750,000 for *The Misfits* (US 61)

Paul Newman $750,000 plus % per film 1965

Spencer Tracy $300,000 for *Guess Who's Coming to Dinner* (US 67)

Shirley Maclaine $800,000 plus % for *Sweet Charity* (US 68)

Dustin Hoffman $425,000 for *John and Mary* (US 69)

☆ *1970s*

Sean Connery $1,200,000 for *Diamonds are Forever* (GB 71)

Charles Bronson $20,000–$30,000 plus $2,500 living allowance per day 1975

Robert Redford $2 million for *A Bridge Too Far* (GB 77)

Robert Redford $3 million per film 1978

Paul Newman $3 million per film 1978

Steve McQueen $3 million per film 1978

Marlon Brando $3,500,000 for featured role in *Superman* (GB 78)

☆ *1980s*

Burt Reynolds $5 million for *The Cannonball Run* (US 81)

43

*Burt Reynolds was paid $5 million for his role in **The Cannonball Run**.*

Dustin Hoffman $4 million for **Tootsie** (US 82)

Sean Connery $5 million for **Never Say Never Again** (GB 83)

Sylvester Stallone $7 million (inc writing and directing) for **Rocky III** (US 83)

Robert Redford $6 million for **Out of Africa** (US 86)

Eddie Murphy following success of **Beverly Hills Cop** (US 84), signed $25 million contract to star in six films for Paramount.

...AND NOT SO WELL

Not all movie salaries are astronomical. Many of today's superstars earned comparatively little in their early days, and even when success comes some stars are prepared to work for a nominal

fee if the project appeals to them. The examples given below of the bottom end of the salary scale need to be viewed in relation to the megabuck fees quoted in the previous list.

☆ **Karen Black** agreed to make the much acclaimed **Can She Bake a Cherry Pie?** (US 83) for a nominal fee of $1,038. She did not even make that. When the Screen Actors Guild found the movie had been made without union approval, they fined Ms Black precisely $1,038.

☆ **James Cagney** played the role of George M. Cohan in **The Seven Little Foys** (US 55) for nothing. He refused a fee out of respect for the memory of Eddie Foy, who had befriended him in his youth.

☆ **Julie Christie** was paid only $7,500 for her Oscar winning performance in **Darling** (GB 65). Many years of fame and fortune later, she starred in a feminist movie called **Gold Diggers** (GB 84) for the same pay as each of the other members of the cast–£30 a day.

☆ **Montgomery Clift**'s agent demanded a six figure fee for him to play the victim of Nazi sterility measures in **Judgement At Nuremberg** (US 61), but the actor decided to do it for nothing in tribute to the persecuted. Afterwards he sent his agent a paper bag containing the commission due to him–it was empty.

☆ **Sean Connery** won the coveted 007 role in the first Bond movie **Dr No** (GB 62) not least because he was cheap–£15,000 at a time when major stars were already attracting up to $1 million for a single film. Not until **Diamonds Are Forever** (GB 71)

*James Cagney played the role of George M. Cohan in **The Seven Little Foys** for nothing.*

years when he was offered $15,000 to appear in a spaghetti western called *A Fistful of Dollars* (It 64). By 1972 he was the No 1 star at the box office and over the last decade his movies have grossed a record $1,400 million.

☆ **Olivia de Havilland** starred in Paramount's *The Well-Groomed Bride* (US 46) for a nil salary because she was in litigation with her home studio, Warner Bros. She could not be paid by another studio, but her agent thought she should do the film for nothing to stay in the public eye.

☆ **Dustin Hoffman** was worth $17,000 for the smash hit *The Graduate* (US 67) and $425,000 a couple of years later for the floppo *John and Mary* (US 69).

☆ **Olivia Hussey** was paid £1,500 for eleven months work when she made her screen debut as Juliet in Zefferelli's *Romeo and Juliet* (GB 68). It was probably rather less than the production secretaries earned.

☆ **Sylvia Kristel**, who claimed to be the highest paid actress in Europe following her success as *Emmannuelle*, agreed to make *Pastorale 43* (Neth 78) in her native Holland for no slary and a nil percentage. It was, she said, a simple matter of tax avoidance.

☆ **Vivien Leigh** was paid $15,000 to play the most coveted role in movie history. The total emolument for her Oscar winning performance as Scarlett in *Gone With the Wind* (US 39) was less than ice-skating star Sonja Henie was then being paid for a single week's work.

☆ Stephen J. Lewicki cast rock star **Madonna** in *A Certain Feeling* (US 84) before she catapulted to overnight fame and

did he find himself up there with them, the only British star in the seven figure league.

☆ **James Dean** was paid $18,000 for his memorable performance in *East of Eden* (US 55). It was his fifth film but his first starring role and it rocketed him to instant stardom.

☆ Perhaps the last of the great western stars, **Clint Eastwood** had already been in movies for nearly ten not very productive congratulated himself all the way to the bank for securing her services at $100 all in.

☆ **Steve McQueen** was paid $3,000 to play the lead in tacky horror movie *The Blob* (US 58). He was not invited to appear in the sequel, *Son of Blob* (US 71). By that time his fee would have been several times the whole budget of the movie.

☆ **Genevieve** (GB 53) was the top British comedy of 1953, but it only boosted Kenneth More's earnings by £3,000.

☆ **Paul Newman** was paid $17,500 each for his Warner Bros pictures of the mid-1950s. In the mid-1960s he was getting $750,000 per film plus a percentage.

☆ **Kim Novak** received her regular salary of $100 a week from Columbia while making *The Man with the Golden Arm* (US 56), though producer Otto Preminger had to pay the studio $100,000 for her services.

☆ **Frank Sinatra** earned $8,000 for his Oscar winning performance in *From Here to Eternity* (US 53). Nodules on his throat had brought his singing career to a temporary halt and he was desperate to get back into movies at any price.

☆ **Sylvester Stallone** claimed that the only remuneration he received for playing a leading role in *The Lords of Flatbush* (US 74) was 25 free T-shirts.

☆ Hollywood's lowest paid contract player of all time was **Robert Taylor**, who signed with MGM for $35 a week in 1934. He never held it against the studio for so undervaluing his services. He stayed with them for 25 years, longer than any other major star.

TOP MONEYMAKING FILM OF EACH DECADE

☆ *1910–19 The Birth of a Nation* (US 15)

☆ *1920–29 The Big Parade* (US 25)

☆ *1930–39 Gone With the Wind* (US 39)

☆ *1940–49 Song of the South* (US 46)

☆ *1950–59 The Ten Commandments* (US 56)

☆ *1960–69 The Sound of Music* (US 65)

☆ *1970–79 Star Wars* (US 77)

☆ *1980–86 E.T. The Extra-Terrestial* (US 82)

MONEY MONEY MONEY

The Nickel Ride (US 74)

Ten Cents a Dance (US 45)

Half Dollar Bill (US 24)

60 Cents an Hour (US 23)

One Silver Dollar (Fr/It 75)

Two Dollar Bettor (US 51)

The $5 Baby (US 22)

$10 Raise (US 35)

$20 a Week (US 74)

$1000 a Minute (US 74)

$5,000 Reward (US 18)

$30,000 (US 20)

100,000 Dollars in the Sun (US 64)

$1,000,000 Duck (US 71)

Billion Dollar Scandal (US 32)

A Thousand Billion Dollars (Fr 82)

PRIVATE PURSUITS

WHEN I GROW UP

Some child stars, like Elizabeth Taylor and Natalie Wood, went on to superstardom. Others, like Jackie Cooper and Jackie Coogan, became character actors. Most left the screen altogether. This list reveals what happened to some of them.

☆ **Baby Jane** (Juanita Quigley) spent 13 years as a nun in Pennsylvania before renouncing her vows in 1964 to become an English teacher at Delaware County Community College and marrying a Professor of Theology at Villanova University, Pa.

☆ **Baby Le Roy**, the infant whose milk was allegedly spiked with gin by the child-hating W. C. Fields, retired from the screen in 1936 aged 4. On leaving school he became a merchant seaman.

☆ **Baby Marie Osborne**, infant star of the silent screen, became a costume designer with credits for *Spartacus* (US 60) and *How to Murder Your Wife* (US 64).

☆ **Baby Peggy** (Peggy Montgomery) became proprietor of a greetings card company.

☆ **Baby Sandy** (Sandra Henville), star of Universal movies of the late 30s and early 40s, became a legal secretary in the office of the County Counsel of Los Angeles.

☆ **Wesley Barry**, freckle-faced teenager in silent pictures, became a turkey farmer.

☆ **Freddie Bartholomew**, English-born star of *David Copperfield* (US 35), *Captain Courageous* (US 37), *Kidnapped* (US 38) etc., became a Vice President of the advertising agency Benton & Bowles.

☆ **Joseph Boudreaux**, the boy who hero-worshipped the oil riggers in *Louisiana Story* (US 48), became an oil rigger.

☆ **John Howard Davies**, star of David Lean's *Oliver Twist* (GB 48), went into television production after leaving films, becoming BBC Head of Comedy in 1977 and BBC Head of Light Entertainment in 1982. He is now a senior producer with Thames Television.

☆ **Deanna Durbin** married French director Charles-Henri David and became chatelaine of the chateau at the village of Neauphle-le-Château, near Paris.

☆ **Peggy Ann Garner**, who received a special Academy Award for her performance in *A Tree Grows in Brooklyn* (US 45), became a car salesman for General Motors.

☆ **Bonita Granville**, nominated for an Academy Award for *These Three* (US 36) at the age of 13, went on to become an adult actress first, then went into TV production. She produced TV's *Lassie* series.

☆ **Billy Halop**, teenage tough

*Would you buy a car from this young lady? After Academy Award recognition for her performance in **A Tree Grows in Brooklyn**, she grew up to become a salesman for General Motors.*

proprietor of East Texas Water Systems and the J & B Beautiful Pig Farm.

☆ **Marcia Mae Jones**, who played Klara in *Heidi* (US 37), became a switchboard operator in a lawyer's office.

☆ **Mark Lester**, Britain's leading post-war boy actor and star of *Oliver!* (GB 68), was working as a barman at the Britannia pub in Kensington in 1985 after beating a drug problem and spending all the money he had earned as a child. He hopes to return to acting.

☆ **Spanky McFarland**, best known of the Our Gang troupe, became a restaurateur, wine salesman and a sales-training supervisor for Philco-Ford.

☆ **Mandy Miller**, star of *Mandy* (GB 52), married an architect and now lives in an 18th-century rectory at Newhaven, Sussex.

☆ **Darwood K. Smith**, the guy in the Dead End Kids pictures, became an electric dryer salesman, then a male nurse.

☆ **Claude Jarman**, tow-haired hillbilly star of *The Yearling* (US 46), became Director of the San Francisco Opera House.

☆ **Gloria Jean**, teenaged singer who became the B picture equivalent of Deanna Durbin, worked as a receptionist for a Van Nuys manufacturing company.

☆ **Jackie 'Butch' Jenkins**, buck-toothed and freckle-faced Huck Finn type who had to retire when he developed a stutter, became

Fame and fortune deserted Mark Lester and he became a barman in a West End pub.

studious Waldo persecuted by Alfalfa in the Our Gang comedies, became a missionary in Thailand.

☆ **Shirley Temple** became US Ambassador to Ghana and Chief of Protocol at the White House. She now instructs newly appointed ambassadors on diplomatic procedure and practice.

☆ **Bobs Watson**, one of the nine Watson children appearing in movies of the 30s, became a Methodist minister at Magnolia Park Church, Burbank.

OFF-SCREEN ACHIEVEMENTS

☆ **Lionel Barrymore** composed a symphony titled *Tableau Russe*, a portion of which was used in *Dr Kildare's Wedding Day* (US 41).

☆ **Florence Bates** became the first woman lawyer in Texas in 1914.

☆ **Wallace Beery** held the world record for the largest black sea bass ever caught, a 515 lbs monster he hooked off Catalina Island in 1916.

☆ **Rex Bell** became Lieutenant Governor of Nevada.

☆ **Chief John Big Tree**, who performed in *Stagecoach* (US 39), *Drums Along the Mohawk* (US 39), *She Wore a Yellow Ribbon* (US 49) etc., was the model for the profile on the Indian Head nickel of 1912.

☆ **Neville Brand** was the fourth most decorated US soldier of World War II.

☆ **Rossano Brazzi** was featherweight boxing champion of Italy.

☆ **Herman Brix**, who played Tarzan under that name but later became known as Bruce Bennett, won the Silver Medal for the shotput at the 1928 Olympics.

☆ **Jim Brown**, a pro-footballer before he became an actor, was voted Athlete of the Year in 1964.

☆ **Lon Chaney** was the author of the *Encyclopaedia Britannica*'s article on theatrical make-up.

☆ **Buster Crabbe**, who played Flash Gordon and other B movie heroes, won the 400 metres freestyle Gold Medal for swimming at the 1932 Olympics.

☆ **Bebe Daniels**, a BBC war correspondent in World War II, was the first female civilian to land in Normandy after D-Day.

☆ **Irene Dunne** was an Alternative Delegate at the 12th Session of the UN General Assembly in 1957.

☆ **Clint Eastwood** was elected Mayor of Carmel, California, in 1986. His first public utterance on taking the oath of office was that there were too many lawyers on the City's payroll. His first act as Mayor was to legalize ice cream parlors.

☆ **Vittorio Gassman** made the Italian national basketball team at the age of 17.

☆ **John Gavin** became US Ambassador to Mexico.

☆ **Sonja Henie**, Fox star of ice musicals, became Norwegian ice skating champion at 14 and world champion at 15, holding her title for 10 years. She was also a Gold Medallist in three successive Olympics.

☆ **Ben Johnson** won the steer-roping world championship in 1953.

☆ **Rafer Johnson** won the Gold Medal for the Decathlon at the 1960 Olympics.

☆ **Victor Jory** was light heavyweight boxing champion of British Columbia.

☆ **James Robertson Justice** was Rector of Edinburgh University. He also taught Prince Charles falconry.

☆ **John Lodge** became Governor of Connecticut in 1950, US Ambassador to Spain in 1955, US Ambassador to Argentina in 1968, US Ambassador to Switzerland in 1979 and US delegate to the UN in 1984.

☆ **Melina Mercouri** became the Greek government's Minister of Arts and Sciences following her election as a MP in 1977.

☆ **Glenn Morris**, star of *Tarzan's Revenge* (US 38), won the Gold Medal for the Decathlon at the 1936 Olympics.

☆ **Audie Murphy** was the most decorated soldier in US history, winning 24 medals from the Congressional Medal of Honor down. He personally killed 240 Germans. His exploits were the subject of *To Hell and Back* (US 55), in which he starred as himself.

☆ **George Murphy** was elected Senator for California.

☆ **Paul Newman** was a delegate to the 1978 UN Conference on Disarmament. He is also a champion motor racing driver and has won the Sports Car Club of America National Championship three times, including the 1985 event.

☆ **Donald O'Connor** has won recognition as a composer of orchestral music. His first symphony was performed by the Los Angeles Philharmonic Orchestra under his own baton.

☆ **Kitty O'Neill**, deaf-mute Cherokee Indian who is the doyenne of Hollywood stunt women, broke the women's land speed record at 618 mph.

☆ **Ronald Reagan** was elected Governor of California in 1966 and 1970 and President of the United States in 1980 and 1984.

☆ **Steve Reeves** won the Mr America, Mr World and Mr Universe titles before making his screen debut in *Athena* (US 54).

☆ **Paul Robeson**, while at Rutgers University, was the first black football player to become an All-American.

☆ **Omar Sharif** represented Egypt in the 1964 Olympic bridge tournament.

☆ **Robert Shaw** won the 1962 Hawthornden Prize for his novel *The Sun Doctor*.

☆ **Robert Stack** held a world record of 351 consecutive hits at skeet-shooting.

☆ **Lou Tellegan**, handsome leading man who starred opposite Sarah Bernhardt in three of her movies, was the model for Rodin's celebrated sculpture *The Kiss*.

☆ **Johnny Weismuller**, the screen's best remembered Tarzan, won two Gold Medals for swimming at the 1924 Olympics and five at the 1928 Olympics.

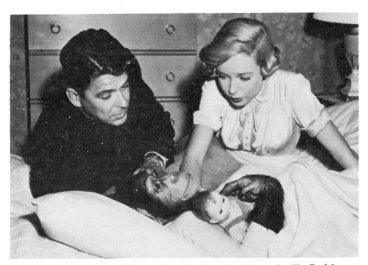

*The fellow on the left decided to quit monkeying about in movies like **Bedtime for Bonzo** and see if he could do any better in politics.*

STARS IN PRINT

Many stars have written their autobiographies, but it is surprising how many have authored other kinds of books as well. This is a selection:

Mary Astor
Image of Kate (novel)
A Place Called Saturday (novel)
etc.

Woody Allen
Getting Even (humorous sketches)
With Our Feathers (humorous sketches)
Side Effects (humorous sketches)

Lionel Barrymore
Mr Cantonwine: A Moral Tale (novel)

Anne Baxter
Intermission (about life in the Australian outback–movie in pre-production)

Joan Blondell
Center Door Fancy (novel)

Dirk Bogarde
A Gentle Occupation (novel)

Voices in the Garden (novel)
West of Sunset (novel)

Richard Burton
A Christmas Story

Leslie Caron
Vengeance (novel)

Diane Cilento
The Manipulator (novel)

Iron Eyes Cody
How Indians Sign Talk and others on Indian lore

Buster Crabbe
The Arthritis Exercise Book

Robert Cummings
How To Stay Young and Vital

Tony Curtis
Kid Andrew Cody and Julie Sparrow (novel)

Arlene Dahl
Always Ask a Man and 11 other beauty books

Errol Flynn
Beam Ends (about a voyage to New Guinea)

Corinne Griffith
Eggs I Have Known (cook book)
Papa's Delicate Condition (about

family life with her inebriate father–played by Jackie Gleason in the 1963 film of the same name)

Jean Harlow
Today Is Tonight (novel)

George Kennedy
Murder on Location (novel)

Herbert Lom
Enter the Spy (about playwright Christopher Marlowe)

Sophia Loren
In the Kitchen with Love (cook book)

Shirley Maclaine
You Can't Get There From Here (travel book on China)

Virginia McKenna
On Playing with Lions (wildlife)
Some of My Friends Have Tails (wildlife)

Colleen Moore
How Women Can Make Money in the Stock Market

David Niven
Once Over Lightly (novel)

Mary Pickford
Why Not Try God (religion)

George Sanders
Stranger at Home (thriller–filmed in 1954 with Paulette Goddard)

Robert Shaw
The Hiding Place (novel)
The Man in the Glass Booth (novel)
The Sun Doctor (novel–winner of Hawthornden Prize 1962)

Simone Signoret
Adieu Volodia (novel)

Elizabeth Taylor
Nibbles and Me (about her pet chipmunk; written aged 12)

Ernest Thesiger
Adventures in Embroidery

Kay Thompson
Eloise (bestselling children's book; character supposedly based on the young Liza Minelli)

Tom Tryon
The Other (occult thriller; filmed in 1972)

Rudolph Valentino
Day Dreams (verse)

Robert Vaughn
The Victims (about the 1950s Hollywood blacklist)

Erich Von Stroheim
The Fires of St John (novel)
Paprika (novel)

Orson Welles
The Lives of Harry Lime (short stories)

Mae West
Diamond Lil (novel; also play of same name)
The Constant Sinner (novel)

Kenneth Williams
Acid Drops (anthology of classic put-downs)

Susannah York
The Last Unicorn (children's story)

Victor Sen Yung
'No 1 Son' in most of the Charlie Chan movies:
The Great Wok Cookbook (Yung was an expert on Chinese cuisine, though he had never visited China).

BEAUTY QUEENS

☆ **Zeenat Aman** (India's No 1 box office star for much of the 70s) Miss Asia 1971

☆ **Claudine Auger** Miss France 1958

☆ **Lauren Bacall** Miss Greenwich Village 1942

☆ **Joan Blondell** Miss Dallas 1929

☆ **Lucia Bose** Miss Italy 1949– also played a Miss Italy in

Antonioni's *Donna Senza Camelie*
(It 53)

☆ **Dyan Cannon** Miss West
Seattle 1957

☆ **Claudia Cardinale** The Most
Beautiful Italian Girl in Tunis 1956

☆ **Jeanne Crain** Miss Long
Beach 1941 (runner-up in Miss
America contest)

☆ **Yvonne de Carlo** Miss
Venice Beach 1941

☆ **Anita Ekberg** Miss Sweden
1951

☆ **Zsa Zsa Gabor** Miss Hungary
1936–disqualified when she was
found to be under 16

☆ **Gila Golan** Miss Israel 1961

☆ **Anne Heywood** Miss Great
Britain 1950

☆ **Shirley Jones** Miss
Pittsburgh 1951

☆ **Sylvia Kristel** Miss Television
Europe 1973

☆ **Veronica Lake** Miss Florida
1937–disqualified when she was
found to be under 16

☆ **Dorothy Lamour** Miss New
Orleans 1931

☆ **Gina Lollobrigida** Miss Italy
1946

☆ **Sophia Loren** Princess of the
Sea 1948; Miss Elegance 1950

☆ **Jayne Mansfield** Miss Photo-
flash 1952

☆ **Vera Miles** Miss Kansas 1948

☆ **Kim Novak** Miss Deepfreeze
1953

☆ **Debbie Reynolds** Miss
Burbank 1948

☆ **Cybill Shepherd** Miss
Teenage Memphis 1966

☆ **Elke Sommer** Miss Viareggio
1959

☆ **Raquel Welch** Miss
Photogenic 1953 (aged 13)

WHAT THEY DID BEFORE …

Chiropody, coalmining, sanitary
engineering, coffin making or
being a gangster or a monk might
not appear the most obvious
stepping stones to stardom, but
they were a means of livelihood
for some of the stars listed below
before the lights of Hollywood
beckoned. It should be noted that
many of these performers had
more than one occupation before
turning to acting; here we have
listed just one for each. Very few
of the new generation of stars
appear; that is because very few of
them have been anything but
actors–a significant development
perhaps? As the most common
route to stardom, at least for the
ladies, has been via modelling or
the chorus, those who started that
way are listed separately.

☆ **Renee Adorée** circus
bareback rider

☆ **Arletty** factory girl

☆ **Harriet Andersson** lift
operator

☆ **Dana Andrews** accountant
with Gulf Oil

☆ **Lauren Bacall** cinema
usherette in Manhattan

☆ **Warren Beatty** rat catcher

☆ **William Bendix** grocer

☆ **Monte Blue** grave digger

☆ **Humphrey Bogart** US Marine

☆ **John Boles** spy with US
intelligence services

☆ **Ernest Borgnine** US Navy

☆ **Clara Bow** doctor's
receptionist

☆ **Peter Boyle** monk

☆ **George Brent** member of IRA

☆ **Cark Brisson** boxer

☆ **Charles Bronson**

Pennsylvania coalminer (at $1 a ton)

☆ **Jim Brown** pro-footballer with Cleveland Bruins

☆ **Joe E. Brown** pro-football player with St Paul

☆ **Edgar Buchanan** dentist– and played dentist in *Texas* (US 41)

☆ **Genevieve Bujold** cinema usherette in Montreal

☆ **James Caan** rodeo rider

☆ **Bruce Cabot** boxer

☆ **Michael Caine** Smithfield meat porter

☆ **Rory Calhoun** boxer

☆ **John Carradine** portrait painter and marine artist

☆ **Madeleine Carroll** schoolmistress in Hove

☆ **Maurice Chevalier** electrician

☆ **Sean Connery** French polisher for coffin maker

☆ **Chuck Connors** pro-baseball player with Los Angeles Angels

☆ **Joseph Cotten** pro-footballer

☆ **Joan Crawford** laundry girl

☆ **Paul Douglas** pro-footballer with Frankford Yellow Jackets, Philadelphia

☆ **Nelson Eddy** switchboard operator

☆ **Edith Evans** milliner

☆ **Douglas Fairbanks** soap manufacturer

☆ **Fernandel** grocer–father was also a grocer and he played a grocer's son in *Le Rossier de Madame Husson* (Fr 32)

☆ **Barry Fitzgerald** civil servant with the Board of Trade

☆ **Errol Flynn** policeman with the New Guinea Constabulary

☆ **Glenn Ford** bus driver

☆ **George Formby** jockey

☆ **Edward Fox** shop assistant

☆ **Alec B. Francis** barrister

☆ **Ronald Fraser** Donald Wolfit's dresser (The egotistical tragedian played by Albert Finney in *The Dresser* (GB 84) is alleged to have been based on Wolfit, but it is unlikely that Tom Courtney's role as his dresser was based on Ronald Fraser.)

☆ **Clark Gable** telephone repairman

☆ **Greta Garbo** barber shop assistant in Stockholm

☆ **Greer Garson** advertising

☆ **Janet Gaynor** cinema usherette

☆ **Edmund Gwenn** lawyer

☆ **John Gilbert** rubber goods salesman

☆ **Sidney Greenstreet** tea planter in Ceylon

☆ **John Gregson** telephone engineer

☆ **Hugh Griffith** bank clerk

☆ **Sir Alec Guinness** advertising copywriter

☆ **Oliver Hardy** cinema manager

☆ **Sterling Hayden** sea captain at age 22

☆ **Michael Hordern** schoolmaster

☆ **Rock Hudson** postman

☆ **John Huston** Mexican cavalry officer

☆ **Lauren Hutton** Playboy Bunny

☆ **Jeremy Irons** social worker

☆ **Glenda Jackson** shop assistant at Boots the Chemists

☆ **Sam Jaffe** mathematics teacher

☆ **Sidney James** worked at South African diamond mine

☆ **Mervyn Johns** dentist

☆ **Alan Ladd** proprietor of hot-dog stand

☆ **Dorothy Lamour** lift operator with Marshall Field of Chicago

☆ **Burt Lancaster** lingerie salesman with Marshall Field of Chicago

☆ **Charles Laughton** hotel clerk

☆ **Jerry Lewis** bellboy–which role he reprised in *The Bellboy* (US 60)

☆ **John Loder** pickle maker

☆ **Peter Lorre** bank clerk

☆ **Tim McCoy** Adjutant General of Wyoming at age 28

☆ **Malcolm McDowell** coffee salesman–and played coffee salesman in *O Lucky Man!* (GB 73)

☆ **Ali MacGraw** editorial assistant on *Harper's Bazaar*

☆ **Victor McLaglen** boxer

☆ **Steve McQueen** fairground barker

☆ **Miles Mander** sheep farmer in New Zealand

☆ **Fredric March** bank clerk

☆ **Herbert Marshall** chartered accountant

☆ **Dean Martin** croupier

☆ **Lee Marvin** plumber's mate

☆ **Walter Matthau** filing clerk

☆ **Burgess Meredith** reporter with the *Cleveland Plain Dealer*

☆ **Robert Mitchum** coalminer

☆ **Marilyn Monroe** stripper at the Mayan burlesque house on Hill Street, Los Angeles (1948)

☆ **Yves Montand** barman

☆ **Robert Montgomery** deck-hand on oil tanker

☆ **Kenneth More** fur-trapper in Canada

☆ **Glenn Morris** pro-footballer with Detroit Lions

☆ **Jack Nicholson** worked in cartoon department at MGM

☆ **Kim Novak** lift operator

☆ **Dan O'Herlihy** architect

☆ **Jack Palance** boxer

☆ **Larry Parks** Inspector on the New York Central Railroad

☆ **Valerie Perrine** stripper in Las Vegas–and played same in *Lennie* (US 74)

☆ **Eric Portman** menswear salesman

☆ **Dick Powell** worked for telephone co.

☆ **William Powell** worked for telephone co. (no connection with above)

☆ **George Raft** worked in protection racket

☆ **Raimu** croupier

☆ **Basil Rathbone** insurance

☆ **Aldo Ray** Constable of Crockett, Calif. (resigned after failing to make any arrests)

☆ **Ronald Reagan** sports announcer on radio–and played radio announcer for first starring role in *Love Is On the Air* (US 37)

☆ **Sir Michael Redgrave** schoolmaster at Cranleigh–and played schoolmaster in *The Browning Version* (GB 51)

☆ **Oliver Reed** bouncer for strip club and played a bouncer in *The Two Faces of Doctor Jekyll* (GB 60)

☆ **Michael Rennie** car salesman

☆ **Burt Reynolds** pro-footballer with the Baltimore Colts

☆ **Sir Ralph Richardson** office boy with insurance co.

☆ **Thelma Ritter** telephone operator

☆ **Roy Rogers** operative in shoe factory

☆ **Jane Russell** chiropodist's assistant

☆ **Margaret Rutherford** piano teacher

☆ **Telly Savalas** worked for State Department

☆ **Randolph Scott** male model

☆ **George Segal** leader of jazz band

☆ **Norma Shearer** cinema pianist

☆ **Jay Silverheels ('Tonto')** pro-lacrosse player in Canada

☆ **Alastair Sim** tailor

☆ **Sylvester Stallone** lion cage cleaner

☆ **Barbara Stanwyck** wrapped packages for a living at age 13 (in 1944 was highest paid woman in America)

☆ **Rod Steiger** civil servant

☆ **Gloria Swanson** shop assistant

☆ **Terry Thomas** grocer

☆ **Fred Thompson** (cowboy star of silents) Presbyterian minister

☆ **Tom Walls** London police constable

☆ **Raquel Welch** cocktail waitress

☆ **Donald Wolfit** prep school master in Eastbourne

☆ **Edward Woodward** worked for sanitary engineer

Chorus Girls
Carroll Baker; Louise Brooks; Ruth Chatterton; Joan Crawford; Arlene Dahl; Marion Davies; Marlene Dietrich; Marie Dressler; Alice Faye; Lilian Harvey; Rita Hayworth; Miriam Hopkins; Betty Grable; Paulette Goddard; Ruby Keeler; Kay Kendall; Carole Landis; Myrna Loy; Jeanette MacDonald; Nita Naldi; Anna Neagle; Barbara Stanwyck.

Model Girls
Brigitte Bardot; Senta Berger; Jacqueline Bisset; Linda Blair (as child); Ellen Burstyn; Dyan Cannon; Capucine; Jeanne Crain; Arlene Dahl; Francoise Dorleac; Lesley-Ann Down (as child); Anita Ekberg; Shirley Ann Field; Susan Hayward; Lauren Hutton; Grace Kelly; Sylvia Kristel; Jessica Lange; Gina Lollobrigida; Sophia Loren; Carol Lynley (as child); Sue Lyon (as child); Ali MacGraw; Dorothy Malone; Silvana Mangano; Elsa Martinelli; Maria Montez; Jennifer O'Neill; Charlotte Rampling; Lee Remick; Dominique Sanda; Lizabeth Scott; Brooke Shields; Simone Simon; Elke Sommer; Alexandra Stewart; Gene Tierney; Cicely Tyson; Tuesday Weld (as child).

... AND AFTER

Most stars retire from the screen rich and do not choose to go on working. Those who do often go into production or some other branch of show business. A few, including those listed below, opt for something completely different. Some chose politics– including the well-known star of *Bedtime for Bonzo*–and they are listed separately under 'Off Screen Achievements'. A surprising number became ordained ministers, monks or nuns, which suggests that the material blessings of Hollywood do not always mean personal fulfilment. And there are others, sadly, who found themselves in menial occupations once Hollywood had withdrawn her favours.

☆ **Art Acord**, top cowboy star of the 20s, became a vagrant.

☆ **Stephanie Bachelor**, black-hearted villainess of 1940s B pictures, became an expert in illuminated Gothic hand-printing.

☆ **Vilma Banky** became a champion golfer.

☆ **John Drew Barrymore** became a hermit in the California desert, living on wild lettuce and sunflower seeds.

☆ **Eva Bartok** became an ordained minister of the Universal Life Church.

☆ **Lina Basquette** became a breeder of Great Danes.

☆ **Smith Bellew**, singing cowboy, worked on guided missiles for Howard Hughes Aircraft Inc.

☆ **Eleanor Boardman** became Paris fashion correspondent for *Harper's Bazaar*.

☆ **Mary Brian**, the 'perpetual ingénue' of the 1930s, became a portrait painter.

☆ **Louise Brooks**, the immortal 'Lulu', became a salesgirl at Saks Fifth Avenue.

☆ **Billie Burke** launched her own brand of salad dressing. (Paul Newman, though still active in pictures, has done the same.)

☆ **Madeleine Carroll** became an apple grower.

☆ **Chester Conklin**, walrus-moustached silent comedian, became a Santa Claus in a Los Angeles department store.

☆ **Betty Compson** became a department store cosmetics demonstrator.

☆ **Edna Mae Cooper** became an evangelist.

☆ **Ricardo Cortez** became a stockbroker.

☆ **Hazel Court**, British star of the 1940s, became a professional painter.

☆ **Donald Crisp** became a banker.

☆ **Buster 'Flash Gordon' Crabbe** became a stockbroker.

☆ **Karl Dane** ran a hamburger stand outside MGM Studios.

☆ **Charles Farrell**, Janet Gaynor's co-star in a dozen pictures, became a professional tennis player.

☆ **Frances Farmer**, after a spell in gaol and years spent in and out of mental institutions, secured work as a receptionist in a San Francisco hotel.

☆ **James Fox** became an evangelist.

☆ **Virginia Gilmore**, 40s leading lady and former wife of Yul Brynner, graduated in Cytology (the study of cells) at the University of Vienna.

☆ **Cary Grant** became a corporate executive with the Rayett-Fabergé cosmetics company.

☆ **Richard Greene** became a horse breeder in Ireland.

☆ **Billy Halop** of the Dead End Kids became a male nurse.

☆ **Juanita Hansen**, Pearl

White's successor as Queen of the Serials, became addicted to drugs, was cured in 1934, and obtained a job as a train order-clerk for the Southern Pacific Railroad.

☆ **Ty Hardin** became an ordained minister at Prescott, Arizona.

☆ **Dolores Hart** became Mother Dolores of the cloistered convent of Regina Laudis at Bethlehem, Conn.

☆ **Lilian Harvey** established a snail farm in France.

☆ **June Haver** entered St Mary's Convent in Xavier, Kansas in 1953 but abandoned her habit six months later to marry Fred MacMurray.

☆ **Sessue Hayakawa**, Hollywood's most enduring oriental actor, became an ordained Zen priest in Japan after retiring in 1960.

☆ **Betty Hutton**, after many tribulations, became a domestic at St Anthony's Rectory in Portsmouth, Rhode Island.

☆ **Veronica Lake**, five times married as well as being courted by Howard Hughes and Aristotle Onassis, became a barmaid in a New York hotel.

☆ **Elissa Landi**, Austrian countess who moved to Hollywood after achieving stardom in British films, became a successful novelist.

☆ **Lash La Rue**, 'King of the Bullwhip', became first a hellfire and brimstone evangelist in a tent-show touring the southern states, then a monk at St Petersburg, Florida.

☆ **Francis Lederer** opened an art gallery in Canoga Park, Calif.

☆ **Gina Lollobrigida** became a successful photo-journalist, pulling off a notable scoop by obtaining an exclusive interview with Fidel Castro.

☆ **Myrna Loy** worked for the United Nations.

☆ **Sue Lyon**, who achieved overnight fame as 'Lolita' when she was 16, became a cocktail waitress at the Ramada Inn, Denver.

☆ **Lamberto Maggiovani**, who played the lead in Vittorio De Sica's *Bicycle Thieves* (It 48), made only one other film and then De Sica set him up in business with a shoe shop in Rome.

☆ **Jessie Matthews** became Mrs Dale of radio's *Mrs Dale's Diary*.

☆ **Jose Mojica**, singing star of Hollywood and Mexican musicals, became a Franciscan Brother in Peru and later an ordained priest.

☆ **Colleen Moore** became a stockbroker on Wall Street.

☆ **George Murphy** manufactured Murphy's Rubbing Linament, using a compound invented by his father.

☆ **Tom Neal**, veteran of 180 pictures and star of *No Greater Love* as leper priest Fr Damien, became a gardener.

☆ **Asta Nielsen**, the first international superstar, became manager of a cinema in Copenhagen.

☆ **Maureen O'Hara** became Vice President of one of the few airlines in the world whose fleet is entirely flying boats, the Antilles Air Boat Co. of the Virgin Islands.

☆ **Maureen O'Sullivan** became an executive director of Wediquette International, a company that provides bridal services.

☆ **Barbara Payton**, star of B pics *Kiss Tomorrow Goodbye* (US 50) and *Bride of the Gorilla* (US 51), became a convicted prostitute.

☆ **Eleanor Powell** became (among other things) a Presbyterian Sunday School teacher.

☆ **Edmund Purdom** became a producer of classical records for RCA Victor.

☆ **George Raft** became a reservation clerk for the River Hotel, Las Vegas.

☆ **Esther Ralston**, known as 'the Paramount Clotheshorse' for her stylish dress, became a lighting consultant with Glens Falls Electrical Supply Co. in Glens Falls, NY.

☆ **Tex Ritter**, singing cowboy, estabished a fast food franchise empire under the name Tex Ritter Chuck Wagons.

☆ **Janice Rule**, leading lady of the 50s and former wife of Ben Gazzara, became a psychoanalyst specialising in members of her earlier profession.

☆ **Jane Russell** founded an adoption agency for US families to adopt foreign children.

☆ **Jay Silverheels**, 'Tonto' of *The Lone Ranger*, became a harness racing driver.

☆ **Penny Singleton**, the featherbrained 'Blondie' of the Blondie and Dagwood series, became a full-time union official with the American Guild of Variety Artists and acquired a reputation as a formidable opponent at the negotiating table.

☆ **Anna Sten**, only actress to have achieved stardom on both the Soviet screen and the Hollywood screen, became a professional painter.

☆ **Russ Tamblyn** became a professional painter.

☆ **Frankie Thomas**, juvenile lead in the Nancy Drew pictures, became a bridge teacher.

☆ **Lawrence Tierney**, who played the title role in *Dillinger* (US 45), became a hard-hat construction worker on a West 57th Street skyscraper and later drove a horse-cab in Central Park.

☆ **Richard Todd** became a dairy farmer.

☆ **Collen Townsend** became an ordained minister.

☆ **Bobs Watson**, child actor, became a Methodist minister.

☆ **Johnny Weissmuller** became a 'greeter' at Caesar's Palace in Las Vegas and proprietor of a health food store in Hollywood.

☆ **Alice White**, petite blonde flapper of the 20s, became a secretary, the same job she had before becoming a star.

☆ **Pearl White**, 'Queen of the Serials', ran a casino in Biarritz.

☆ **Claire Windsor**, major star of the silent era, became manager of a fishing fleet.

☆ **Jane Wyman**, the ex-Mrs Reagan, became a professional painter.

STARS WHO HAVE SERVED TIME

☆ Cowboy star **Art Accord** was gaoled in 1929 for bootlegging. It ended his career.

☆ **Arletty**, incomparable star of *Les Enfants du Paradis* (Fr 44), spent two months in gaol after the Liberation of Paris for her liaison with a German officer. She had been condemned to death by a Free French tribunal in Algiers in 1944.

☆ **Harry Baur**, star of *Un Carnet de Bal* (Fr 37), was imprisoned and tortured by the Gestapo for forging papers to prove Aryan origins. He died in mysterious circumstances a few days after his release in 1943.

☆ **Matthew 'Stymie' Beard**, the little black boy in a Derby in the *Our Gang* comedies, was sentenced to ten years for drug pushing after his screen career had ended at the age of 18.

☆ **Rory Calhoun** served three years in Springfield State Prison for car theft.

☆ **Pierre Clementi**, star of *Belle de Jour* (Fr 67), was imprisoned in Italy in 1972 on a charge of drug possession but released unconvicted after being on remand for 17 months.

☆ French comedian **Coluche** was sentenced to two months in gaol in June 1985 for insulting a police officer.

☆ Former child star **Bobby Driscoll**, who played Jim Hawkins in *Treasure Island* (US 50), was imprisoned in 1961 for carrying drugs.

☆ **Bebe Daniels** was sentenced to ten days in gaol in 1921 for speeding. Her next movie, *The Speed Girl* (US 21), was about a movie star who goes to gaol for speeding.

☆ **Frances Farmer** was given a 180-day sentence in 1943 for breaking probation after a drunk-driving charge. On being sentenced she flung an ink-pot at the judge's head.

☆ In 1920s New Guinea **Errol Flynn** was sentenced to two weeks in gaol for hitting a Chinaman who had presumed to address him by his surname without the prefix 'Mr'. As there was no gaol for white men, he was consigned to the care of a man called Tom Price who was in charge of prisoners. He passed the time playing poker with his gaoler and escaping into the town every night for more carnal activities.

Flynn's next spell in custody was at Salamaua, New Guinea in 1929 on a charge of murdering a Kanaka. He conducted his own defence and was acquitted when the prosecution was unable to produce the body of the deceased.

In 1933 Flynn found himself in gaol in Djibouti, capital of French Somaliland, for hitting a customs officer.

His next spell in chokey lasted only one night. A New York policeman had forced Flynn's car off the road and demanded his autograph in what the star considered a menacing manner. On being taken down to the station, he stamped on the cop's instep and was promptly beaten up and thrown into a cell.

☆ **Juliette Greco** was imprisoned by the Germans at age 15 when her mother and sister were deported to Germany.

☆ **Stacy Keach** served six months in Reading Gaol in 1984–5 for attempting to smuggle £4,500 worth of cocaine into Britain.

☆ **Paul Kelly** served time at San Quentin following his conviction in 1927 for the slaying of the husband of actress Dorothy Mackaye. He married the lady on his release. Many years later he returned to San Quentin, though on screen only, playing the title role of the warden in **Duffy of San Quentin** (US 54).

☆ **Sophia Loren** served a month in a Rome gaol in 1982 for income tax irregularities.

☆ **Steve McQueen** spent two years at a Californian reform school called the Boys' Republic in the late 1940s. As a US Marine he spent 41 days of his service in detention.

☆ **Robert Mitchum** was sentenced to a Georgia chain gang at Savannah in 1933 when he was 16. The prosecution failed to pin a theft charge on him as he was able to prove to the judge that he was already in gaol on the day the robbery took place. The judge in a fit of pique restored the original charge of vagrancy and handed him an indeterminate sentence. He escaped after seven days.

In 1948, when he was already a star, Mitchum served 59 days in a California gaol for possession of narcotics.

☆ **Tom Neal**, handsome MGM leading man of the 30s, was convicted of involuntary manslaughter of his third wife in 1965 and served seven years at the California Institution for Men at Chino.

☆ **Ivor Novello** served a month in Wormwood Scrubs when he was convicted of obtaining petrol unlawfully during World War II.

☆ **Johnny Popwell**, black actor who played a youth sent to prison in Georgia for assault with a deadly weapon in **The Heart Is a Lonely Hunter** (US 68), received a real-life sentence in 1975 of 10 years' gaol for a street shooting in Atlanta, Ga.

☆ Romanian-born **Duncan Renaldo**, who achieved fame as the 'Cisco Kid', served eight months on McNeil Island for illegal entry to the USA in 1932. He was released on being granted a Presidential Pardon by Franklin Delano Roosevelt.

☆ **Tommy Rettig**, child star of the 50s, was sentenced to 5½ years in a Federal Prison in 1976 for smuggling cocaine from Peru.

☆ **Jay Robinson**, who played Caligula in **The Robe** (US 53), was convicted on a drugs charge in 1967 and served 15 months.

☆ **Jane Russell** was gaoled for drunken driving in 1978.

☆ **Phil Silvers** was sent to PS 61 Reform School in Brooklyn for allegedly attacking his teacher. He claimed that it was a fix–all he had done was say, 'Why don't you?', when she threatened to jump out of the window and pushed her away when she dug her skeletal fingers into his arm.

☆ **Mae West** was sentenced to ten days on Welfare Island in 1926 when her first Broadway stage production, **Sex**, was declared to be obscene. She got two days' remission for good behaviour.

Note **Gina Lollobrigida** was sentenced to a two months suspended gaol sentence and a fine of 40,000 lire (£23) by a Rome court in 1966 for appearing in a film, **The Dolls** (It 66), declared to be obscene. She was bound over not to appear in any more obscene movies for five years.

MARRIAGE LINES

WHO MARRIED WHOM

Stars who married stars. An asterisk indicates divorce.

Brian Aherne–Joan Fontaine*

Anouk Aimée–Albert Finney*

June Allyson–Dick Powell*

Annabella–Tyrone Power*

Fatty Arbuckle–Minta Durfee*

Dezi Arnaz–Lucille Ball*

Renee Asherson–Robert Donat

Richard Attenborough–Sheila Sim

Stephane Audran–Jean-Louis Trintignant*

Jean-Pierre Aumont–Maria Montez*

Lew Ayres–Lola Lane*; Ginger Rogers*

Lauren Bacall–Humphrey Bogart; Jason Robards*

Anne Bancroft–Mel Brooks

Vilma Banky–Rod La Rocque

Lex Barker–Arlene Dahl*; Lana Turner*

John Barrymore–Dolores Costello*

Eva Bartok–Curt Jurgens*

Wallace Beery–Gloria Swanson*

Richard Benjamin–Paula Prentiss

Constance Bennett–Gilbert Roland*

Jacques Bergerac–Ginger Rogers*; Dorothy Malone*

Edna Best–Herbert Marshall*

Joan Blondell–Dick Powell*

Claire Bloom–Rod Steiger*

George Brent–Ruth Chatterton*; Constance Worth*; Ann Sheridan*

Charles Bronson–Jill Ireland

Coral Browne–Vincent Price

Virginia Bruce–John Gilbert*

Richard Burton–Elizabeth Taylor*
Elizabeth Taylor*

Dyan Cannon–Cary Grant*

Madeleine Carroll–Sterling Hayden*

Charlie Chaplin–Paulette Goddard*

Ina Claire–John Gilbert*

Sir John Clements–Kay Hammond

Lew Cody–Mabel Normand

Joan Collins–Anthony Newley*

Ronald Colman–Benita Hume

Jackie Coogan–Betty Grable*

Joseph Cotten–Patricia Medina

Joan Crawford–Douglas Fairbanks Jr*; Franchot Tone*

Richard Cromwell–Angela Lansbury*

Tony Curtis–Janet Leigh*

Lili Damita–Errol Flynn*

Bebe Daniels–Ben Lyon

Bobby Darin–Sandra Dee*

John Derek–Ursula Andress*; Linda Evans*; Bo Derek

Betsy Drake–Cary Grant*

Clint Eastwood–Sondra Locke

Anita Ekberg–Anthony Steel*

Britt Ekland–Peter Sellers*

Denholm Elliott–Virginia McKenna*

Jill Esmond–Laurence Olivier*

Douglas Fairbanks Sr–Mary Pickford*

Mia Farrow–Frank Sinatra*

Mel Ferrer–Audrey Hepburn*

Henry Fonda–Margaret Sullavan*

Bryan Forbes–Nanette Newman

Glenn Ford–Eleanor Powell*

Anthony Franciosa–Shelley Winters*

Lynne Frederick–Peter Sellers

Fiona Fullerton–Simon MacCorkindale*

Magda Gabor–George Sanders*

Zsa Zsa Gabor–George Sanders*

Ava Gardner–Mickey Rooney*; Frank Sinatra*

Greer Garson–Richard Ney* (played her son in *Mrs Miniver*)

Vittorio Gassman–Shelley Winters*

Susan George–Simon MacCorkindale

John Gilbert–Leatrice Joy*; Ina Claire*; Virginia Bruce*

Paulette Goddard–Charlie Chaplin*; Burgess Meredith*

Elliott Gould–Barbra Streisand*

Stewart Granger–Jean Simmons*

Cary Grant–Virginia Cherill*; Dyan Cannon*; Betsy Drake*

Richard Greene–Patricia Medina*

Richard Harris–Ann Turkel*

Rex Harrison–Lilli Palmer*; Kay Kendall; Rachel Roberts*

Laurence Harvey–Margaret Leighton*

Rita Hayworth–Orson Welles*

David Hemmings–Gayle Hunnicutt*

Benita Hume–Ronald Colman; George Sanders*

Jill Ireland–David McCallum*; Charles Bronson

Hattie Jacques–John Le Mesurier*

Richard Johnson–Kim Novak*

Al Jolson–Ruby Keeler*

Jennifer Jones–Robert Walker*

Buster Keaton–Natalie Talmadge*

Rachel Kempson–Sir Michael Redgrave

Hedy Lamarr–John Loder*

Fernando Lamas–Arlene Dahl*; Esther Williams

Jessica Lange–Sam Shepard

Vivien Leigh–Sir Laurence Olivier*

Margaret Leighton–Laurence Harvey*; Michael Wilding

Carole Lombard–William Powell*; Clark Gable

Ben Lyon–Bebe Daniels; Marian Nixon

John McCallum–Googie Withers

Simon MacCorkindale–Fiona Fullerton*; Susan George

Ali MacGraw–Steve McQueen*

Virginia McKenna–Denholm Elliott*; Bill Travers

Dorothy Malone–Jacques Bergerac*

Patricia Medina–Richard Greene*; Joseph Cotten

Yves Montand–Simone Signoret

Dudley Moore–Suzy Kendall*; Tuesday Weld*

Owen Moore–Mary Pickford*

Paul Newman–Joanne Woodward

Sir Laurence Olivier–Jill Esmond*; Vivien Leigh*; Joan Plowright

Peter O'Toole–Sian Phillips*

Geraldine Page–Rip Torn

Lilli Palmer–Rex Harrison*; Carlos Thompson

Mary Pickford–Owen Moore*; Douglas Fairbanks*; Buddy Rogers

Sidney Poitier–Joanna Shimkus

Ronald Reagan–Jane Wyman*

Mickey Rooney–Ava Gardner*; Lana Turner*

George Sanders–Zsa Zsa Gabor*; Benita Hume*; Magda Gabor*

George C. Scott–Trish Van Devere

Janette Scott–Mel Torme*

Peter Sellers–Britt Ekland*; Lynne Frederick

Robert Shaw–Mary Ure

Frank Sinatra–Ava Gardner*; Mia Farrow*

Maggie Smith–Robert Stephens*

Barbara Stanwyck–Robert Taylor*

Elizabeth Taylor–Michael Wilding*; Richard Burton*; Richard Burton*

Lupe Velez–Johnny Weissmuller*

Robert Wagner–Natalie Wood*; Natalie Wood

Michael Wilding–Elizabeth Taylor*; Margaret Leighton

Shelley Winters–Vittorio Gassman*; Anthony Franciosa*

Grant Withers–Loretta Young*

*Of the marriages listed above, 74% ended in divorce.

⌐□□□□□□□□□□□□□□□□□□□□□□⌐

FOR BETTER OR WORSE

Some facts about Hollywood marriage and divorce

☆ The most married stars in the Hollywood galaxy have been Lana Turner, Mickey Rooney, Zsa Zsa Gabor, Stan Laurel and Georgia Holt, each with eight marriages. The latter two hold the record for most repeat marriages to the same person, with Georgia Holt marrying John Sarkisian, the father

of Cher, three times, and Stan Laurel marrying Virginia Rogers three times.

☆ Mickey Rooney said: 'I'm the only man who has a marriage licence made out To Whom It May Concern.'

☆ Seven times married Elizabeth Taylor said: 'What do you expect me to do? Sleep alone?'

☆ At her sixth marriage, Miss Taylor was asked by the registrar for the names of her previous husbands. The Queen of Hollywood fixed him with a baleful eye. 'What's this,' she asked, 'a memory test?'

☆ In 1938 *Motion Picture Magazine* conducted a survey which showed that divorce was almost twice as prevalent among Hollywood stars as among other Americans. At a time when just over 16% of American marriages ended in divorce, 29% of married stars from Hollywood's 'Top 400' had divorced at least once. Of the 313 who had been married:

212 claimed to have been married only once (71%)
 63 claimed to have been married twice (20%)
 24 claimed to have been married three times (8%)
  5 claimed to have been married four times or more (1.5%)

Only 194 children were claimed by these 'Top 400' stars, and of these 19 had been adopted.

☆ Things appear to have got worse rather than better following World War II. Dr Robert L. Sumner, a Southern Baptist minister, focused attention on the sorry state of matrimony in the movie capital with a computation that in 1949 there were 42 marriages

Husband and wife team Grant Withers and Loretta Young decided they had been too young to marry after co-starring in **Too Young to Marry***. Child-bride Loretta was just 17.*

involving a prominent screen star and 180 divorces.

☆ The most oft-quoted reason for the brief span of so many Hollywood marriages is that busy show business couples seldom see each other. It is rare for an erstwhile marriage partner to fail to recognise their former spouse, but it has been known. Visiting a night club, forties leading lady Martha Stewart ran into comedian Joe E. Lewis, the husband she had divorced after two years of marriage, and greeted him warmly. After he had said goodbye, Lewis turned to a friend at the bar and asked: 'Who was that beautiful girl?'

☆ Lack of maturity is often a contributory factor. Grant Withers and Loretta Young were divorced shortly after co-starring in the aptly titled **Too Young to Marry** (US 31). They had been married in 1930 at ages 25 and 17 respectively.

☆ Eva Bartok was only 15 when she married for the first time and she claims that her first three marriages were unconsummated. The initial disaster was to an SS officer in Hungary; her next was a marriage of convenience to film producer Alexander Paal simply in order to get out of Hungary. The third was to film publicist William Wordsworth, a descendant of the poet, and she parted from him at the wedding ceremony.

☆ Eva Bartok may well hold the record for the shortest marriage partnership, but a number of other stars are close. Jean Acker left Rudolph Valentino on their wedding night in 1920. Silent star Dagmar Godowsky was equally disenchanted with her second husband. Immediately after the ceremony he put his arm round her possessively and asked: 'Who do you belong to now?' Dagmar had no desire to belong to anyone. 'I couldn't stand it,' she recalled. 'I had him take me for dinner and after that I said goodbye.'

☆ No star contracted marriages with greater frequency than tragic 'good time girl' Barbara La Marr. When she died alone of heroin addiction at the age of 29 she had already been married six times.

☆ Happily some Hollywood marriages do last. Will Rogers said: 'I'm not a real movie star–I've got the same wife I started out with 28 years ago.'

☆ Hollywood's most enduring marriage was between James Cagney and his wife Frances, who were a dancing duo in vaudeville before making the partnership permanent. They celebrated their Diamond Wedding on 28 September 1982 and were parted only by Cagney's death in 1986 after 63 years of marriage.

MOST MARRIAGES

☆ Married 4 times
Anouk Aimée
Lionel Barrymore
William Boyd
Yul Brynner

Richard Burton
Madeleine Carroll
Jack Carson
Charlie Chaplin
Joan Collins
Chester Conklin
Jackie Coogan
Joan Crawford
John Derek
Rhonda Fleming
Joan Fontaine
Paulette Goddard
Al Jolson
Peter Lorre
Mae Murray
Merle Oberon
George Sanders
Margaret Sullavan
Michael Wilding
Gig Young

☆ Married 5 times
Lex Barker
Eva Bartok
George Brent
Paul Douglas
Henry Fonda
Clark Gable
Judy Garland
Rita Hayworth
Veronica Lake
John Loder
Herbert Marshall
Victor Mature
Ginger Rogers
Gloria Swanson

☆ Married 6 times
Rex Harrison
Barbara La Marr
Hedy Lamarr
Johnny Weissmuller

☆ Married 7 times
Claude Rains
Elizabeth Taylor

☆ Married 8 times
Zsa Zsa Gabor
Georgia Holt
Stan Laurel
Mickey Rooney
Lana Turner.

STARS WHO MARRIED NON-ACTING CELEBRITIES

☆ Dawn Addams married Prince Vittorio Massimo.

☆ Barbara Bach married Ringo Starr.

☆ Catherine Deneuve married photographer David Bailey.

☆ Mia Farrow married conductor André Previn.

☆ Paulette Goddard married novelist Erich Maria Remarque.

☆ Cary Grant married Woolworth heiress Barbara Hutton.

☆ Laurence Harvey married top model Paulene Stone.

☆ Rita Hayworth married Prince Aly Khan.

☆ Valerie Hobson married Defence Minister John Profumo.

☆ Rosamund John married Government Chief Whip and later Minister of Agriculture John Silkin.

☆ Jennifer Jones married multi-millionaire art collector Norton Simon.

☆ Grace Kelly married Prince Rainier of Monaco.

☆ Sue Lyon ('Lolita') married Gary 'Cotton' Adamson in 1973 at Colorado State Penitentiary, where he was serving 20–40 years for murder and armed robbery.

☆ Marilyn Monroe married playwright Arthur Miller.

☆ Patricia Neal married novelist Roald Dahl.

☆ Anny Ondra, leading lady of the first British talkie, Hitchcock's **Blackmail**, married world heavyweight boxing champion Max Schmeling.

☆ Jean Peters married reclusive tycoon Howard Hughes–during their 14 years of marriage no photo of them together was ever published, and only one of her alone (by *Life* in 1969 showing Mrs Hughes at the opera in Los Angeles).

☆ Moira Shearer married broadcaster Ludovic Kennedy.

HOLLYWOOD'S BACHELORS

Very few stars have remained unmarried. Even the gay members of the Hollywood community have tended to make marriages of convenience. Rock Hudson, for example, married his secretary at his manager's insistence to allay rumours about his sexual orientation. Listed below are the Hollywood and British stars who chose to remain single.

Warren Beatty
Dirk Bogarde
Montgomery Clift
Noel Coward
Farley Granger
Tab Hunter
Sal Mineo
Ramon Novarro
Ivor Novello
Cesar Romero
Terence Stamp
Ernest Thesiger
Anton Walbrook
Kenneth Williams

Julie Christie
Lillian Gish
Greta Garbo
Valerie Perrine
Mary Philbin
Flora Robson
Lizabeth Scott
Simone Simon
Anna May Wong

HOLLYWOOD THE WORLD OVER

NATIONAL ORIGINS

Not all the stars were what fans may have assumed them to be.

☆ Character actress **Joyce Grenfell**, arch exponent of the dotty English spinster, was indeed born in England, but was American on both sides of her family. Her mother was Nancy Astor's sister.

☆ **Laurence Harvey** was Lithuanian. He was born Laruska Mischa Skikne at Yoniskis in 1928.

☆ **Leslie Howard**, embodiment of the English gentleman to audiences of the 30s and 40s, was of Hungarian parentage and brought up speaking only German.

☆ **Audrey Hepburn** was born in Brussels in 1929 of an Irish father and a Dutch mother, the Baroness Ella van Heemsta.

☆ **Olivia Hussey**, real name Olivia Osuna, is an Argentinian born in Buenos Aires in 1951. Her mother is English.

☆ **Al Jolson** was Russian, born at St Petersburg (now Leningrad) in 1886.

☆ **Anna Magnani** may have been Egyptian. She was born in Alexandria in 1905 of an Italian mother; her father is unknown.

☆ **Adolphe Menjou** may have been Americans' idea of a Frenchman, but he was born in Pittsburgh in 1890.

☆ **Carmen Miranda** was known as 'The Brazilian Bombshell'; in fact she was born at Marco de Canavezes, Portugal, in 1909.

☆ **Yves Montand** was Italian. He was born 1921 at Monsummano, son of an Italian socialist who fled the country when Mussolini came to power.

☆ **Jeanne Moreau** is half English: her mother was a Lancashire chorus girl.

☆ **Merle Oberon** was not an Aussie girl from Tasmania as she purported; she was born in Colombo of a Singhalese mother and brought up in Poona and Bombay. Her racial origin was kept a closely guarded secret until after her death–it would have finished her career in the days when inter-racial romance was taboo on screen.

☆ Professional cad **George Sanders** was of Russian origin, born at St Petersburg in 1906 of a Russian father and English mother.

☆ **Simone Signoret** was German. Born at Wiesbaden in 1921, her real name was Kaminker.

☆ During the flag-waving war years when **Elizabeth Taylor** was getting established as a child star in Hollywood, MGM laid great stress on her English birth. The British were delighted to accept the winsome child, and later the glamorous superstar, as one of themselves, but in reality both her parents were American.

She may have been called 'The Brazilian Bombshell' but in reality Carmen Miranda was Portuguese.

☆ **Edward G. Robinson** was one of the few Romanians to make it big in Hollywood; born Bucharest 1893.

HOLLYWOOD'S BRITS

Brian Aherne (1902–86)
b King's Norton, Worcs

Jacqueline Bisset (1944)
b Weybridge, Surrey

Clive Brook (1887–1974)
b London

Lionel Atwill (1885–1946)
b Croydon

Madeleine Carroll (1906)
b West Bromwich

Charles Chaplin (1889–1977)
b London

Joan Collins (1933)
b London

Ronald Colman (1891–58)
b Richmond, Surrey

Olivia de Havilland (1916)
b Tokyo

Robert Donat (1905–58)
b Withington, Manchester

Joan Fontaine (1917)
b Tokyo

Reginald Gardiner (1903–80)
b Wimbledon

Greer Garson (1908)
b Co Down, N. Ireland

Leo Genn (1905–78)
b London

Stewart Granger (1913)
b London

Cary Grant (1904)
b Bristol

Sydney Greenstreet (1879–1954)
b Sandwich, Kent

Edmund Gwenn (1875–1959)
b Glamorgan

Bob Hope (1904)
b Eltham, Middx

Leslie Howard (1893–1943)
b Forest Hill, London

Boris Karloff (1887–1969)
b Dulwich

Deborah Kerr (1921)
b Helensburgh, Scotland

Esmond Knight (1906)
b East Sheen, Surrey

Elsa Lanchester (1902)
b Lewisham

Angela Lansbury (1925)
b London

Charles Laughton (1899–1962)
b Scarborough

Stan Laurel (1890–1965)
b Ulverston, Lancs

Ida Lupino (1918)
b London

Herbert Marshall (1890–1966)
b London

James Mason (1909–1985)
b Huddersfield

Roddy McDowall (1928)
b London

Victor McLaglen (1883–1959)
b Tunbridge Wells

Ray Milland (1905–1985)
b Neath, Wales

David Niven (1909–1983)
b Kirriemuir, Scotland

Claude Rains (1889–1967)
b London

```
□□□□□□□□□□□□□□□□□□□□□□□
```

HOLLYWOOD'S CANADIANS

Estelle Brody (1904)
b Montreal

Genevieve Bujold (1942)
b Montreal

Jack Carson (1910–63)
b Carman, Manitoba

Yvonne de Carlo (1922)
b Vancouver, B.C.

Marie Dressler (1869–1934)
b Coburg, Ont.

Deanna Durbin (1921)
b Winnipeg

Glenn Ford (1916)
b Quebec

Michael J. Fox (1962)
b Vancouver, B.C.

John Ireland (1914)
b Vancouver, B.C.

Victor Jory (1902–82)
b Dawson City, Yukon

Ruby Keeler (1909)
b Halifax, N.S.

Alexander Knox (1907)
b Ontario

Florence Lawrence (1886–1938)
b Hamilton, Ont.

Gene Lockhart (1891–1957)
b London, Ont.

Raymond Massey (1896)
b Toronto

Douglass Montgomery (1909–66)
b Brantford, Ont.

Barbara Parkins (1942)
b Vancouver, B.C.

Mary Pickford (1893–1979)
b Toronto

Walter Pidgeon (1897)
b East St John, N.B.

Christopher Plummer (1927)
b Toronto

Marie Prevost (1898–1937)
b Sarnia, Ont.

Michael Sarrazin (1940)
b Quebec City

William Shatner (1911)
b Montreal

Norma Shearer (1900–83)
b Montreal

Joanna Shimkuss (1943)
b Halifax, N.S.

Alexis Smith (1921)
b Peniction, B.C.

Alexandra Stewart (1939)
b Montreal

Donald Sutherland (1935)
b St John, N.B.

Fay Wray (1907)
b Alberta

B.C. = British Columbia
N.C. = Nova Scotia
N.B. = New Brunswick

THOSE UNITED STATES

The names of the United States constantly recur in movie titles. The most common is Texas, which has been used in 104 titles to date, followed by Arizona, with a more modest 49. (Both have tended to fall out of favour since the virtual demise of the western.) The list below gives a single title for each state. If one allows that the name 'Carolina' covers both North and South Carolina, and that 'Dakota' may equally be interpreted as North or South, then there are only eight states which have yet to make it onto a movie theatre marquee. The missing ones are Delaware, Iowa, Massachusetts, New Jersey, Rhode Island, Washington, West Virginia and Wisconsin.

Morgen in Alabama (W. Ger 84)

North to Alaska (US 60)

Arizona Bushwackers (US 68)

Arkansas Traveler (US 38)

California Suite (US 75)

Carolina Moon (US 40)

Colorado Ambush (US 51)

Christmas in Connecticut (US 45)

Down Dakota Way (US 49)

Florida Special (US 36)

The Night the Lights Went Out in Georgia (US 81)

Blue Hawaii (US 66)

The Duchess of Idaho (US 50)

Abe Lincoln in Illinois (US 39)

The Boy from Indiana (US 50)

Kansas Raiders (US 50)

Kentucky Fried Movie (US 77)

Louisiana Story (US 48)

Maine Ocean (Fr 85)

Pride of Maryland (US 51)

The Michigan Kid (US 47)

The Great Northfield, Minnesota Raid (US 72)

Mississippi Triangle (US 84)

The Great Missouri Raid (US 50)

Montana Territory (US 52)

The Nebraskan (US 53)

West of Nevada (US 36)

Hotel New Hampshire (US 84)

Sons of New Mexico (US 49)

New York, New York (US 77)

Glück aus Ohio (Ger 33)

Oklahoma Crude (US 73)

The Oregon Trail (US 59)

Penn of Pennsylvania (GB 41)

Tennessee Champ (US 54)

The Best Little Whorehouse in Texas (US 82)

Utah Wagon Train (US 51)

Moonlight in Vermont (US 43)

Heart of Virginia (US 48)

Green Grass of Wyoming (US 48)

JOURNEYS BY RAIL

Movies about trains are too

innumerable to list. These are movies which took place mainly or wholly *aboard* trains.

Shanghai Express (US 32) British officer (Clive Brook) and former love (Marlene Dietrich) meet on a train which is waylaid by Chinese bandits.

Rome Express (GB 32) Conrad Veidt, Hugh Williams, Sir Cedric Hardwicke and lots of skulduggery aboard the Paris–Rome express in one of the first British movies to make an impact in America.

Twentieth Century (US 34) Carole Lombard is a temperamental actress courted, for professional reasons, by John Barrymore as they ride the eponymous train.

Moskau-Shanghai (Ger 36) Pola Negri's German comeback film, a melodrama set aboard the train to China.

The Lady Vanishes (GB 38) Perhaps the classic British meller of the 30s, with Michael Redgrave and Margaret Lockwood investigating the mysterious disappearance of an old lady on a train travelling from England to Switzerland. Hitchcock par excellence.

The Silent Battle (GB 39) Rex Harrison as a French secret agent who stops Balkan revolutionaries from blowing up a train with the French President aboard.

Night Train to Munich (GB 40) Rex Harrison as a British agent posing as a Nazi officer to save a Czech inventor and his daughter.

Sleeping Car to Trieste (GB 48) Remake of *Rome Express* (see above) with David Tomlinson and Jean Kent.

Törst (Swe 50) Early Bergman. Erotic goings-on between Eva Henning and Birger Malmsten during a train journey from Zurich to Stockholm.

Train to Tombstone (US 50) Don Barry in a movie about a stick-up man's plans to rob a baggage car of $250,000 in gold during the journey to Tombstone.

The Tall Target (US 51) Dick Powell as Abraham Lincoln's ex-bodyguard (discredited when he uncovered a plot to kill the President) on board a train to Baltimore desperately trying to thwart the assassin's intent.

The Narrow Margin (US 52) Prosecution witness, widow of a racketeer, on board a train from Chicago to Los Angeles is in peril from those who are determined she shall not arrive.

Night Train to Paris (GB 64) Catherine Carrel helps an ex-OSS agent save a tape recording from spies.

The Train (US/Fr/It 64) Burt Lancaster, somewhat improbably cast as a French resistance hero, seeks to prevent evil Nazi Paul Scofield from getting a train-load of art treasures to Germany.

Trans-Europ Express (Fr 67) Sex, sadism and smuggling with Jean-Louis Trintignant and delectable victim Marie-France Pisier.

Murder on the Orient Express (GB 74) Belgian detective Hercule Poiret (Albert Finney) solves murder on a snowbound train full of glitterati.

The Cassandra Crossing (US 77) Sophia Loren, Richard Harris, Ava Gardner and Burt Lancaster aboard a plague-stricken trans-

European express.

Rheingold (W. Ger 78) Murder on the Rheingold Express as it speeds across Germany to Basel.

The Lady Vanishes (GB 79) Remake of the '38 classic (see above) with Elliott Gould and Cybill Shepherd bringing some good ol' American know-how to the murder mystery business.

Avalanche Express (US 79) Robert Shaw as high-ranking Soviet defector being transported across Europe by CIA agents, with constant attacks on the train by grim-faced Russkies.

Terror Train (Can 80) Jamie Lee Curtis and other assorted teenagers are menaced by a psycho-on-the-loose during a train excursion. (Why didn't they get off?)

Maine Ocean (Fr 85) Rosa Maria Gomes as a young Brazilian woman travelling on the Maine Ocean Express from Paris to Nantes without a valid ticket–and what befalls her.

Runaway Train (US 85) Jon Voight as an escaped convict fleeing on a train which runs out of control in the Alaskan wilderness when the driver dies.

HOME TOWN

Most of the world's big cities and many of the smaller ones have been used in movie titles. This list is confined to titles which consist only of the names of towns.

Abilene Town (US 46)

Alburquerque (US 48)

Atlantic City (US 44) (Can/Fr 81)

Bagdad (US 49)

Baton-Rouge (Fr 85)

Bengazi (US 55)

Benghazi (It 42)

Berlin (Ger 27)

Bilbao (Sp 78)

Birdsville (Aus 86)

Cairo (GB 42) (GB 63)

Calcutta (US 47)

Canon City (US 48)

Carson City (US 52)

Casablanca (US 42)

Casablanca, Casablanca (It 85)

Cheyenne (US 47)

Chicago (US 27)

Coronado (US 35)

Dallas (US 50)

Dimboola (Aus 79)

Dodge City (US 39)

El Paso (US 49)

Fort Worth (US 51)

Guadalajara (Mex 43)

Havre (Fr 86)

Honolulu (US 39)

Houston, Texas (Fr 81)

Istanbul (US 57) (Belg 84)

Khartoum (GB 66)

Lahore (India 53)

Laramie (US 49)

Lisbon (US 56)

London (GB 26)

Malacca (Swe 86)

Malaga (GB 54)

Manaos (It/Mex/Sp 80)

Mandalay (US 34)

Maracaibo (US 58)

Marbella (It 86)

Miami (US 24)

Monte Carlo (US 26) (US 30)

Montevideo (W. Ger 52) (W. Ger 64)

Naples and Sorrento (It 30)

Nashville (US 75)

New Orleans (US 29) (US 47)

New York (US 16) (US 27)

New York, New York (US 77)

Palm Beach (Aus 79)

Palm Springs (US 36)

Paris (US 26) (US 29)

Paris, Texas (W. Ger 84)

Paris–New York (Fr 40)

Port Arthur (Cz 37)

Port Said (US 48)

Prague (Cz 85)

Quebec (US 51)

Reno (US 23) (US 30) (US 39)

Rio (US 39)

Saigon (US 48)

San Antonio (US 45)

San Francisco (Belg 83)

Santiago (US 56)

Santa Fe (US 51)

Shanghai (US 35)

Sofia (US 48)

Suddenly (US 54)–Calif.

Talpa (Mex 57)

Tangier (US 46)

Teheran (GB 47)

Texas City (US 52)

Timbuctoo (GB 33)

Timbuktu (US 59)

Tobruk (US 66)

Tombstone (US 42)

Tucson (US 49)

Tulsa (US 49)

Union City (US 80)

Valencia (Ger 27)

Valparaiso, Valparaiso! (Fr 71)

Vera Cruz (US 54)

Virginia City (US 40)

Washington (Iran 83)

Wetherby (GB 85)

Wichita (US 55)

STREET WISE

☆ LONDON

The Seer of Bond Street (GB 13)

A Park Lane Scandal (GB 15)

The Girl from Downing Street (GB 18)

The Man from Downing Street (US 22)

The Lonely Lady from Grosvenor Square (GB 22)

No 5 John Street (GB 22)

A Window in Piccadilly (GB 28)

Piccadilly (GB 29)

Piccadilly Nights (GB 30)

Greek Street (GB 30)

77 Park Lane (GB 31)

Berkeley Square (US 33)

The Barretts of Wimpole Street (US 34)

Charing Cross Road (GB 35)

Hyde Park Corner (GB 35)

Laburnum Grove (GB 36)

Piccadilly Playtime (GB 36)

Piccadilly Jim (US 36)

East of Ludgate Hill (GB 37)

The Black Sheep of Whitehall (GB 41)

East of Piccadilly (GB 41)

The Man in Half Moon Street (US 44)

I Live in Grosvenor Square (GB 45)

Waterloo Road (GB 45)

Piccadilly Incident (GB 46)

The Courtneys of Curzon Street (GB 47)

Bond Street (GB 48)

Spring in Park Lane (GB 48)

It Happened in Leicester Square (GB 49)

The Lavender Hill Mob (GB 49)

23 Paces to Baker Street (US 56)

The Barretts of Wimpole Street (GB 57)

The Siege of Sidney Street (GB 60)

Piccadilly Third Stop (GB 60)

10 Rillington Place (GB 70)

Mad Mission III: Our Man from Bond Street (W. Ger 85)

Half Moon Street (GB 86)

Basil of Baker Street (US 86)

84 Charing Cross Road (GB 86)

☆ **PARIS**

77 Rue Chalgrin (US 31)

The King of the Champs-Elysées (Fr 35)

Remontons les Champs-Elysées (Fr 38)

13 Rue Madeleine (US 46)

125 Rue Montmatre (Fr 59)

Quai Notre-Dame (Fr 61)

Women of the Bois du Boulogne (Fr 64)

122 Rue de Provence (Fr 78)

La Place de la Bastille (Neth 84)

☆ **NEW YORK**

Tenth Avenue (US 28)

81st Street (US 28)

Broadway (US 29)

Wall Street (US 29)

42nd Street (US 33)

East of 5th Avenue (US 33)

The House on 56th Street (US 33)

The Girl from 10th Avenue (US 35)

Times Square Playboy (US 36)

15 Maiden Lane (US 36)

Park Avenue Logger (US 37)

52nd Street (US 37)

10th Avenue Kid (US 38)

Fifth Avenue Girl (US 39)

Wall Street Cowboy (US 39)

The Mayor of 44th Street (US 42)

Clancy Street Boys (US 43)

Murder in Times Square (US 43)

The Phantom of 42nd Street (US 47)

The House on 92nd Street (US 45)

It Happened on 5th Avenue (US 47)

Miracle on 34th Street (US 47)

10th Avenue Angel (US 48)

Park Row (US 52)

Slaughter on Tenth Avenue (US 57)

Madison Avenue (US 62)

Fleshpot on 42nd Street (US 72)

Across 110th Street (US 72)

The Prisoner of Second Avenue (US 74)

Hester Street (US 75)

Times Square (US 80)

East 103rd Street (US 83)

NB The 50 or so titles containing the name 'Broadway' have been omitted.

BABBLE OF TONGUES

The first, and sometimes only, film made in the following languages:

Armenian *Pepo* (USSR 35)

Breton *Lo Pais* (Fr 73)

Esperanto *Incubus* (US 65), starring William Shatner.

Frysian (language spoken in part of North Holland) *De Droom* (Neths 85)

Gaelic *Hero* (GB 82), directed by Barney Platts-Mills.

Icelandic *Milli fjalls og fjöru* (Iceland 48)

Irish *Poitin* (Eire 78), starring Cyril Cusack as poteen distiller.

Latin *Sebastiane* (GB 76), homo-erotic biopic of St Sebastian, directed by Derek Jarman.

Maltese *Katarin* (Malta 77)

Mongolian *Son of Mongolia* (USSR 36)

Okinawan (language of Okinawa in the Ryukyu Is) *Paradise View* (Jap 85)

Pidgin English *Wokabout Bilong Tonten* (Aus 73)

Red Indian *Windwalker* (US 80), starring Trevor Howard. Made entirely in Cheyenne and Crow languages.

Sanskrit (the Indian classical language–no longer spoken) *Sankaracharya* (India 82)

Welsh *The Last Tasmanian* (Aus/GB/Fr 79)

Yiddish *Style and Class* (US 29), starring Goldie Eisenman and Marty Baratz.

Zulu *U'Deliwe* (SA 75).

The Americans have been turning out films in foreign languages ever since Bryan Foy directed *The Royal Box* in German for Warner Bros in 1929. Spanish is the only minority language in which movies are regularly produced in the USA, but here are a few of the languages less often spoken in America which have made it to the screen:

Armenian *Tears of Happiness* (US 74)–a musical

Chinese *Golden Gate Girl* (US 41)

Japanese *Mishima* (US 85)

Serbo-Croat *Ljubar I Strast* (US 32)–it means *Love and Passion.*

Britain does not make many foreign language films, but worthy of note is the first British production in Hindi, the Cabana Film Co.'s 1978 comedy-thriller *Bhaag Re Bhaag*; and the first Chinese language movie, *Ping Pong* (GB 86), a comedy thriller starring David Yip and set in London's Chinatown, made in Cantonese.

AROUND THE WORLD

One title per country. All these films are features, not travelogues.

Afghanistan–Days of Hell (It 86)

The Conquest of Albania (Sp 83)

Candlelight in Algeria (GB 43)

Once Upon a Time in America (US 84)

Antarctica (Jap 84)

Made in Australia (Aus 75)

Bahama Passage (US 41)

Barbados Quest (GB 56)

If It's Tuesday, This Must Be Belgium (US 69)

Bermuda Mystery (US 44)

East of Borneo (US 31)

The Boys from Brazil (US 78)

The Bulgarian Night (Fr 71)

Objective Burma (US 45)

The Canadians (US 61)

A Night Over Chile (USSR 71)

The China Syndrome (US 79)

Cold in Colombia (W. Ger 85)

Drums of the Congo (US 42)

Carnival in Costa Rica (US 47)

Cuba Crossing (US 80)

Denmark Closed Down (Den 80)

Chan in Egypt (US 35)

Tell England (GB 35)

Girl of Finland (Fin 68)

The Foreman Went to France (GB 41)

Souvenir of Gibraltar (Bel 75)

Germany Pale Mother (W. Ger 79)

Guyana–Cult of the Damned (Mex/Sp/Panama 79)

Haiti Express (Den 83)

Hulda from Holland (US 16)

Appointment in Honduras (US 53)

The Man from Hong Kong (US 75)

The Hungarians (Hun 78)

Iceland (US 42)

A Passage to India (GB 85)

Adventures in Iraq (US 43)

Doughboys in Ireland (US 43)

Moon of Israel (US 27)

A High Wind in Jamaica (GB 62)

Escapade in Japan (US 57)

Fair Wind to Java (GB 52)

A Hill in Korea (GB 56)

A Yank in Libya (US 42)

Macao (US 52)

Malaya (US 49)

Malta Story (GB 57)

Thunder Over Mexico (US 33)

Son of Mongolia (USSR 36)

Montenegro (Swe/GB 81)

Morocco (US 30)

Mozambique (GB 64)

The Birth of New Zealand (NZ 22)

Nicaragua–No Pasaran (Aus 84)

The Man from Niger (Fr 40)

Song of Norway (US 70)

Rififi in Panama (Fr 66)

La Guerra de Paraguay (Bra 86)

The Birds will Die in Peru (Fr 68)

The Women of Pitcairn Island (US 57)

Lenin in Poland (USSR 66)

Song of Russia (US 43)

Napoleon at Saint Helena (Fr 29)

On the Isle of Samoa (US 50)

Lo Sconosluto di San Marino (It 48)

Bonnie Scotland (US 35)

Anna and the King of Siam (US 46)

Sierra Leone (W. Ger 86)

The Diary from South Africa (Neth 82)

Flight from Singapore (GB 62)

Contraband Spain (GB 55)

Swiss Made (Swz 69)

East of Sudan (GB 64)

Taiwan Canasta (Yug 85)

Tahiti Nights (US 45)

Tanganyika (US 54)

Storm Over Tibet (US 52)

Two Yanks in Trinidad (US 42)

En Venezuela es la Cosa (Ven 78)

A Yank in Vietnam (US 64)

The Belle of North Wales (GB 12)

West of Zanzibar (GB 54)

FASHION AND THE MOVIES

TREND SETTERS

In the days when most people went to the cinema at least once a week, movies were among the foremost arbiters of fashion. Every woman wanted to look like a star— or at least dress like one. Men, too, could be influenced by what they saw on screen, as some of the examples below will testify.

☆ False eyelashes were invented by D. W. Griffith in order to give Seena Owen's eyes an abnormally large and lustrous appearance in her role as Princess Beloved in *Intolerance* (US 16). They were made by a wigmaker who wove human hair through the warp of a strip of exceptionally thin gauze.

☆ Bessie Barriscale caused a sensation with the backless evening gown she wore in *Josselyn's Wife* (US 19) and soon the middle classes were aping a fashion formerly displayed only by their betters.

☆ The general acceptance of soft collars was the result of silent heart-throb Wallace Reid wearing one in a 1922 movie. There was an immediate slump in stiff collars and few Americans under middle age ever wore one again.

☆ The fashion for bobbed hair swept America and Europe after Collen Moore had displayed her shorn locks in *Flaming Youth* (US 23).

☆ The use of mascara and other eye make-up was directly inspired by the example of Theda Bara and Pola Negri, who darkened their eye-lids to give themselves an air of mystery in the vamp roles both specialised in during their late teens and early 20s.

☆ Sometimes a star can inspire the revival of a fashion started by an earlier star. It was Garbo's much photographed off-screen wearing of berets that started a fashion cult in the 1930s; and it was Faye Dunawaye's portrayal of 30s gangster girl Bonnie Parker in *Bonnie and Clyde* (US 67) that brought back berets in the 1960s.

☆ Even more pervasive in the 1930s was the style inspired by Garbo's Eugenie hat which she wore in *Romance* (US 33). The film may have been set in the 1850s, but to women who had but recently been liberated from the confines of the cloche, a hat which slanted rakishly across the forehead had such appeal that it set the basic configuration of women's headgear for the remainder of the 30s.

☆ Women everywhere took to wearing slacks after Marlene Dietrich wore them in *Morocco* (US 30). Few of her imitators grasped that director von Sternberg had put Dietrich in trousers to emphasise the lesbian characteristics of the role she was playing.

☆ The costume Adrian designed for Joan Crawford in *Today We Live* (US 33) started the vogue for tailored suits with padded shoulders. She herself was so enamoured of the style that she went on wearing them long after they had passed out of fashion.

☆ Plucked eye-brows became the rage about 1930 after Jean Harlow had hers trimmed into a slender arch. Beauty editors advised her imitators to dab ether on their brows to ease the pain of plucking out the hairs.

☆ Men's undershirt sales took a dive after Clark Gable took off his shirt in *It Happened One Night* (US 34) to reveal a bare and rugged torso.

☆ What we now regard as the standard leather biker costume only became so after Brando had appeared looking butch and menacing in zip-up jacket in *The Wild One* (US 54). It also inspired the leather look among gays.

☆ Tropical fabrics became the rage after Dorothy Lamour had appeared in her sarong for the first time in *Jungle Princess* (US 36). The Latin-American look followed, courtesy of Barbara Stanwyck in *The Lady Eve* (US 41); and Jennifer Jones ushered in the Oriental look with her performance in *Love Is a Many Splendored Thing* (US 55).

☆ James Dean's windcheater in *Rebel without a Cause* (US 55) and Elvis Presley's tight trousers in *Jailhouse Rock* (US 57) set the teenage style of the later 1950s and early 1960s.

☆ Footwear is less often influenced by the movies, but girls with slim ankles took to wearing slip-ons without socks or stockings after Bardot had sloughed off the conventions of the formal fifties in *And God*

James Dean's windcheater established a teenage fashion cult in the mid-1950s.

Created Woman (Fr 57). The Sex Kitten also made going barefoot acceptable–she seldom wore shoes off-screen–provided you were young and pretty.

☆ Blonde streaks in brunette hair was a fashion inspired by Audrey Hepburn in *Breakfast at Tiffany's* (US 61).

☆ Wearing dark glasses indoors became a trend after Audrey Hepburn had looked bewitching in them in *Two For The Road* (GB 66).

☆ Jane Fonda's knee-length white vinyl boots in Barbarella (Fr/It 67) became part of the uniform of the mini skirt generation.

☆ Whatever it may or may not have done for the butter industry, *Last Tango in Paris* (Fr/It/US 72) inspired frizzy hair, as exemplified

*Vinyl boots became the rage among the Chelsea set after Jane Fonda had sported them in **Barbarella**.*

by sultry Maria Schneider, and gave permanent waving a new lease of life.

☆ The other kind of casual look, for highbrows rather than hoydens, involved wearing the kind of baggy, rumpled clothes sported by Annie Hall with neurotic chic in **Annie Hall** (US 77). Youth and good looks were not really sufficient if you wanted to get away with this; a certain fey and anxious charm was also imperative.

☆ Off-screen, Yul Brynner wore nothing but black for the last 45 years of his life. He explained: 'I don't have any choices to make in the morning and shopping becomes so much easier.'

CLOTHED ...

The Green Cloak (US 15)
Miss Petticoats (US 16)
Skirts (US 16)
Skinner's Dress Suit (US 17)
The Lilac Sunbonnet (GB 22)
Petticoat Loose (GB 22)
Rolled Stockings (US 27)
An Italian Straw Hat (Fr 27)
Yellow Stockings (GB 28)
Pyjamas Preferred (GB 32)
Top Hat (US 35)
Overcoat Sam (GB 37)
White Tie and Tails (US 46)
The Man in the White Suit (GB 51)
The Green Glove (US 52)
The Red Beret (GB 53)
The Green Scarf (GB 54)
The Bespoke Overcoat (GB 54)
The Man in the Grey Flannel Suit (US 56)
The Fuzzy Pink Dressing Gown (US 57)
Woman in a Dressing Gown (US 57)
The Girl in Black Stockings (US 57)
Woman in a Fur Coat (Swe 57)
The Duke Wore Jeans (US 58)
The Overcoat (USSR 59)
The Crimson Kimono (Jap 59)
The Red Culottes (Fr 63)
Sindrella and the Golden Bra (US 64)
The Dress (Swe 65)

Three Hats for Lisa (GB 65)

The Yellow Hat (GB 66)

Operation Air Raid: Red Muffler (S. Kor 66)

The Green Berets (US 68)

All Neat in Black Stockings (GB 68)

Borsalino (Fr 70)

The Woolen Stocking Peddler (Den 71)

The Girl with the Red Scarf (Tur 78)

Fedora (Fr/W. Ger 78)

The Girl in Yellow Pyjamas (It 78)

The Red Pullover (Fr 79)

The Girl with the Golden Panties (Sp/Ven 80)

Zoot Suit (US 81)

Naughty Blue Knickers (Fr 81)

A Black Gown for a Killer (Fr 81)

The Glove (US 81)

The Persian Lamb Coat (It 82)

Jeans and a T-Shirt (It 82)

Trenchcoat (US 83)

She'll Be Wearing Pink Pyjamas (GB 85)

□□□□□□□□□□□□□□□□□□□□□□□

... AND SHOD

The Bloodstained Shoe (GB 14)

Shoes (US 16)

Little Shoes (US 17)

Wooden Shoes (US 17)

The Shoes That Danced (US 18)

Mrs Lefingwell's Boots (US 18)

Boots (US 19)

Two Little Wooden Shoes (GB 20)

High Heels (US 21)

Another Man's Boots (US 22)

White Slippers (GB 24)

Soft Shoes (US 25)

Old Shoes (US 25)

Rubber Heels (US 27)

Broken Shoes (USSR 33)

Boots! Boots! (GB 34)

Boots of Destiny (US 37)

Boots and Saddle (US 37)

Slipper Episode (US 38)

Tight Shoes (US 41)

They Died With Their Boots On (US 41)

The Bride Wore Boots (US 46)

I Wouldn't Be in Your Shoes (US 48)

The Red Shoes (GB 48)

The Shoes of the Fisherman (US 68)

The Green Shoes (GB 68)

The Sandal (GB 69)

The Computer Wore Tennis Shoes (US 69)

Gumshoe (GB 71)

The Big Blonde Guy With a Black Shoe (Fr 72)

The Woman With Red Boots (Fr/Sp 74)

The Slipper and the Rose (GB 76)

The Tree of Wooden Clogs (It 78)

The Unknown Soldier's Patent Leather Shoes (Bul 79)

Blue Suede Shoes (GB 80)

Sneakers (Can 81)

Alligator Shoes (Can 81)

The Satin Slipper (Fr/Por 85)

Italian Mocassins (Fr 85)

High Heels (Arg 85)

The Man With One Red Shoe (US 85)

BODY TALK

HOLLYWOOD'S BOSOMS

Bosoms came late to the cinema screen, none of the stars actually exploiting their frontal assets as a box office lure before Jean Harlow revealed what a low-cut gown can show in about 1930. Shape was considered more important than size until Howard Hughes began indulging his breast fetish on screen when he cast the 'mean, moody and magnificent' Jane Russell in his notorious film *The Outlaw* (US 43). About the same time Lana Turner was finding fame as 'The Sweater Girl', but as the list below reveals, she was very modestly proportioned. Hollywood's champion bosom of all time belonged to Chesty Morgan, who displayed all 73 inches of it in *Deadly Weapons* (US 75). Jayne Mansfield, among the most generously proportioned of the 'name' stars, could hardly compete, though as Alan King observed: 'She'll never drown.'

- ☆ **34 inches** Lana Turner
- ☆ **35 inches** Bo Derek; Brigitte Bardot
- ☆ **36 inches** Elizabeth Taylor; Ava Gardner; Betty Grable; Zsa Zsa Gabor; Raquel Welch
- ☆ **36½ inches** Rita Hayworth; Ann-Margret
- ☆ **37 inches** Sophia Loren; Marilyn Monroe; Jacqueline Bisset
- ☆ **39 inches** Jane Russell
- ☆ **39½ inches** Jayne Mansfield
- ☆ **40 inches** Dolly Parton

Miss Parton's measurement must be regarded as no more than a conservative estimate. She herself will only admit to her bust being 'somewhere in the low forties'. When pressed on the point by an importunate pressman, she declared: 'That's my secret. But when women's lib started I was the first to burn my bra and it took three days to put out the fire.'

PERSONAL APPEARANCES

☆ **Peter Falk**'s lopsided expression is due to losing his right eye at the age of three from the effects of a tumour. Another actor who wears a glass eye is **Rex Harrison**.

☆ **Herbert Marshall** had only one leg, having lost the other in World War I.

☆ As a young adult **Elizabeth Taylor** was claimed to have Hollywood's slenderest waist–at 21 ins. (Jane Russell's, by comparison, was nearly 27 ins.)

☆ **Marlene Dietrich** achieved her classic sunken cheeks by having her upper rear molars removed.

☆ **Lana Turner** has no eyebrows. Sam Goldwyn had them shaved off for *The Adventures of Marco Polo* (US 38) and they never grew again.

☆ **Laird Cregar** was the shortest

Sexy Rexy. Can you tell which eye is the glass one?

of six brothers–and he stood at 6 ft 3 ins.

☆ **Brando**'s broken nose–he never had it straightened–was given to him by Jack Palance. He hit Brando accidentally while they were larking about backstage during the 1947 run of the stage play *A Streetcar Named Desire*.

☆ **Larry Parks**' legs were of different lengths and he wore a built-up shoe on the shorter one.

☆ **Jack Hawkins**' last film speaking in his own voice was *The Poppy Is Also a Flower* (GB 68). After that he had to have his larynx removed due to throat cancer and learned to speak again through his oesophagus, ten words at a time. He continued to appear in films until his death in 1973, a mimic being employed to dub a voice indistinguishable from Hawkins' own.

☆ **Ronald Reagan** has been deaf since a fellow actor let off a gun next to his ear while they were on set.

☆ **Harold Lloyd**'s famous

glasses–they were an on-screen device only–cost 75c at an optician's on Spring Street, Los Angeles. The first film in which he wore them was *Over the Fence* (US 17).

☆ The first of Hollywood's pretty girls to venture out of doors bare-legged was blonde starlet **Rita Carewe** in 1927. To preserve the proprieties, however, Miss Carewe had her legs *polished* to give the impression she was wearing silk stockings.

☆ **Colleen Moore**, delightful flapper girl of the 20s, had one blue eye and one brown.

☆ During the statutory rape case against **Errol Flynn**, it was alleged that the errant swashbuckler was wont to make love with his socks on. The fact that one of his most recent pictures was titled *They Died With Their Boots On* (US 41) gave a field day to the ribald.

☆ **Gayle Hunnicut** attended a speech clinic to have her Texan accent eliminated. **Evelyn Keyes**, who came from Port Arthur, Texas, worked equally hard at losing her Dixieland twang. Having achieved it, she won her first screen role–playing a Southern belle in Cecil B. De Mille's *The Buccaneer* (US 38); to be followed by another mint julep part as Scarlett's sister in *Gone With the Wind* (US 39).

☆ **Elmo Lincoln**, the first screen Tarzan, claimed to have 'the largest chest in Hollywood'–it measured 53 ins expanded.

☆ **Jeffrey Hunter** was instructed to shave his armpits for his role as Christ in *King of Kings* (US 61).

☆ **Andy Devine**'s rasping voice was occasioned by pushing a metal curtain rod through the roof of his mouth as a child.

☆ **Arletty** had become blind when she played a sighted role as the madame of a brothel in *Les Valets Fermes* (Fr 72).

☆ **Bogey**'s scarred lip was the result of a smash in the mouth by the manacled hands of a prisoner he was transporting during World War I. He shot the man with a .45 automatic.

☆ **Joan Crawford**'s body and face were completely covered in freckles.

☆ **Walter Brennan**, triple Oscar-winning character actor, had no teeth after losing them all in an accident in 1932.

☆ The bandage **Yul Brynner** wore on his finger in *The Journey* (US 59) had nothing to do with the story-line. He had recently jilted a girl in Hollywood who had followed him to Vienna, where the film was shot, and attempted to stab him in the stomach with a knife. He sustained the finger wound defending himself.

☆ Many stars have been victims of their own publicity, but few in such a literal sense as **Harold Lloyd**. While shooting *Haunted Spooks* (US 20), he was posing for a publicity picture with what he thought was a fake prop bomb when it proved to be no fake. The resulting explosion lost him part of his hand, including thumb and forefinger, and he usually played with gloves on thereafter.

☆ **Marilyn Monroe**'s sexy bottom wiggle was occasioned by the fact that she had weak ankles and bandy legs. Realising that these apparent disadvantages were doing her nothing but good, she further accentuated her characteristic walk by sawing a quarter of an inch off the right heel of all her shoes.

☆ **Joan Bennett** was a famous blonde star of the 30s . . . and a famous brunette star of the 40s.

☆ During the making of *Gone With the Wind* (US 39), Vivien Leigh gave an ultimatum that she would refuse to play any more love scenes with **Clark Gable** unless he remedied the foul odour from his dentures.

☆ The roster of actresses who have had face-lifts would be far too long for inclusion here. Actors who have resorted to the same means of preserving their looks include **Gary Cooper**, **Henry Fonda**, **Dean Martin** and **Frank Sinatra**.

☆ **Margaret Dumont** and **Ida Lupino** were both bald and wore wigs. **Carol Channing** also adopted a wig after ruining her hair with constant bleaching. **John Wayne** lost all his hair after contracting a virus in Korea and wore a wig on screen from then on. **Burt Reynolds** also wears one, as well as elevator shoes to compensate for his lack of inches. **John Travolta** has not had to resort to a hairpiece yet, but it is reported from Hollywood that he is spending $50 a day on lotions and restorers to combat a rapidly receding hairline.

☆ Too much hair can be as much of a problem as too little. **Veronica Lake**'s 'peek-a-boo bang' was so much imitated by wartime factory girls, and was the cause of so many industrial accidents, that the US Government asked Paramount to give her a new hairstyle until after the war was over.

Clark Gable's bat-wing ears were a gift for cartoonists.

☆ **William Boyd**'s distinctive white hair–particularly striking in his black Hopalong Cassidy get-up–was not dyed. His hair turned white when he was 29.

☆ **Katherine Hepburn** had an obsession about dirty hair. According to Hollywood columnist Sheilah Graham, when she was at 20th Century Fox she would go around the set sniffing people's hair to make sure it had been washed.

☆ **Lupe Velez**, the Mexican Spitfire, had the unusual ability to rotate her left breast while the other remained static. Moreover she could counter-rotate it, a feat which an appreciative Errol Flynn described as 'so supple and beautiful you couldn't believe your eyes'.

☆ **Judy Garland** wore a latex nose bridge to improve the appearance of her snub nose.

☆ In his earlier pictures **Bing Crosby** had his prominent bat-wing ears stuck back with a special spirit gum. When he attained superstar status he thought, 'What the heck!' and let them resume their natural posture.

☆ But the most celebrated ears in Hollywood undoubtedly belonged to **Clark Gable**. Howard Hughes said they 'made him look like a taxicab with both doors open'.

☆ When Columbia sought a new face to play the lead of the boxer-cum-violinist in *Golden Boy* (US 39), they specified the following attributes for their ideal candidate:

1 Tyrone Power's hair
2 Errol Flynn's forehead
3 Charles Boyer's eyes
4 Wayne Morris's nose
5 Cary Grant's chin
6 Joel McCrea's jaw contour
7 Robert Taylor's mouth
8 Franchot Tone's smile

The fortunate young man who got the job was a 20-year-old unknown who had never appeared on

*William Holden was reckoned to embody the best features of eight major stars when as a 20-year-old unknown he was chosen to play the lead opposite Barbara Stanwyck in **Golden Boy**.*

screen before. Perhaps even more fortunate was the studio to have chosen **William Holden**.

ANATOMY OF THE MOVIES

Bred in the Bone (US 15)
Babbling Tongues (US 17)
Bare Fists (US 19)
Slim Shoulders (US 22)
Backbone (US 23)
Bobbed Hair (US 25)
Silk Legs (US 27)
By the Skin of His Teeth (US 31)
The Big Brain (US 33)
Get Off My Foot (GB 35)
The Accusing Finger (US 36)
Adam's Rib (US 49)
Belles on Their Toes (US 52)
The Screaming Skull (US 58)
Bottoms Up (GB 60)
Arm in Arm, Down the Street (Arg 66)
The Big Mouth (US 67)

The Ankle Bone (Fr 68)
The Hand (Fr 69)
Bearded General (S. Kor 69)
Cutting Heads (Sp/Br 70)
Face (Hun 70)
Trip Around My Cranium (Hun 70)
Clair's Knee (Fr 70)
From Ear to Ear (Fr 70)
Deep Throat (US 72)
Fire to the Lips (Fr 73)
The Pain in the Neck (Fr 73)
Blood in the Streets (US 74)
The Mustard Is in My Nose (Fr 74)
Big Thumbs (US 77)
American Torso (Hun 77)
Pelvis (US 77)
Eyes of Laura Mars (US 78)
The Frozen Heart (Swz/W. Ger/Aust 80)
Somebody's Stolen the Thigh of Jupiter (Fr 80)
The Skin (It/Fr 82)
False Eyelashes (Sp 82)

ROLE REVERSALS

ACTRESSES WHO HAVE PLAYED MEN

There have been many examples of films in which female characters disguised themselves in male attire and in silent days it was not infrequent for young women to play boys, but few actresses have played adult males. Those who have:

☆ **Francesca Bertini** in the title role of *Histoire d'un Pierrot* (It 13).

☆ **Mathilde Comont** as the Persian prince in *The Thief of Bagdad* (US 24).

☆ **Elspeth Dudgeon** (billed as 'John Dudgeon') as the aged man in the upstairs bedroom in *The Old Dark House* (US 32).

☆ **Signe Hasso** as 'Mr Christopher', Nazi agent masquerading as a woman, in *The House on 92nd Street* (US 45).

☆ **Virginia Engels** as old man who falls down the stairs during saloon brawl in *San Antonio* (US 45).

☆ **Sena Jurinac** as Octavian in *Der Rosenkavalier* (GB 62).

☆ **Ivy Ling Po** as the hero Chang in *The Mermaid* (HK 66).

☆ **Caroline Johnson** as the Prince of Denmark in *Hamlet* (Can 71).

☆ **Anne Heywood** as Roy, a transsexual man, in *I Want What I Want* (GB 72).

☆ **Victoria Abril** as an effeminate young man who undergoes a sex change in *I Want To Be a Woman* (Sp 77).

☆ **Linda Hunt**, 4 ft 9 in (1.5 m) American actress, as the male Eurasian cameraman Billy Kwan in *The Year of Living Dangerously* (Aus 82).

☆ **Eva Mattes** as a male film director based on Rainer Werner Fassbinder in *A Man Like Eva* (W. Ger 83).

☆ **Gillian Jones** as Sebastian (also Viola) in *Twelfth Night* (Aus 86).

DRAG ARTISTES

The preceding list is of actresses who have played male roles. There are very few examples of the reverse–actors playing female roles–but quite a few of actors appearing in drag. This list includes examples of both.

☆ **Wallace Beery** as a clumsy Swedish housemaid in the *Sweedie* comedy series of 1912–14.

☆ **Charlie Chaplin** in *A Woman* (US 15).

☆ **Sydney Howard** as the headmistress in *Girls Please!* (GB 34).

☆ **Joe E. Brown** in *Shut My Big Mouth* (US 42).

☆ **Lou Costello** in *Lost in a Harem* (US 44).

☆ **Jerry Lewis** in *At War with*

*War bride Cary Grant in **I was a Male War Bride** with Ann Sheridan.*

the Army (US 44).

☆ **Cary Grant** in *I Was a Male War Bride* (US 49).

☆ **Alec Guinness** as Lady Agatha D'Ascoyne in *Kind Hearts and Coronets* (GB 49).

☆ **Jean Cocteau** as an old woman in *Orphée* (Fr 50).

☆ **Cyril Cusack**, **Stewart Granger** and **Robert Newton** in and as *Soldiers Three* (US 51).

☆ **Bob Hope** in *The Lemon Drop Kid* (US 51).

☆ **Lionel Jeffries** as gem thief posing as headmistress in *Blue Murder at St Trinians* (GB 57).

☆ **Alastair Sim** as the headmistress in *The Belles of St Trinians* (GB 54) and *Blue Murder at St Trinians* (GB 57).

☆ **Tony Curtis** and **Jack Lemmon**, hiding from the Mafia by dressing as members of a girls' band, in *Some Like It Hot* (US 59).

☆ **Anthony Perkins** as psychotic murderer posing as own mother in *Psycho* (US 60).

☆ **Danny Kaye** as 'Marlene Dietrich' in *On the Double* (US 61).

☆ **Hanns Lothar** in *One Two Three* (US 62).

☆ **Dudley Moore** as a nun in *Bedazzled* (GB 67).

☆ **T. C. Jones** as both husband and wife in *The Name of the Game is Kill* (US 68).

☆ **Yul Brynner** singing *Mad About the Boy* to Roman Polanski in *The Magic Christian* (GB 70).

☆ **Peter Sellers** as Queen Victoria in *The Great McGonagall* (GB 72).

☆ **Max Gillies** as an English journalist penetrating an Australian girls-only pre-wedding party in *Dimboola* (Aus 79).

☆ **Michael Caine** as a bewigged murderer in *Dressed to Kill* (US 80).

☆ **George Hamilton** as Zorro's make-believe sister in *Zorro, the Gay Blade* (US 81).

☆ **Philippe Vuillemin** as real-life 19th-century French schoolmistress who changed sex in *The Alexina Mystery* (Fr 85).

☆ **Dom Deluise** as Aunt Kate in *Haunted Honeymoon* (US 86).

FILM STARS PLAYED BY OTHERS

Diana Barrymore by Dorothy Malone in *Too Much Too Soon* (US 58)

John Barrymore by Errol Flynn

in *Too Much Too Soon* (US 58); by Jack Cassidy in *W. C. Fields and Me* (US 76)

Humphrey Bogart by Jerry Lacey in *Play It Again, Sam* (US 72); by Guy Marks in *Train Ride to Hollywood* (US 75); and by Kevin O'Connor in *Bogie* (US 80)–TVM

Eddie Cantor by Buddy Doyle in *The Great Ziegfeld* (US 36); by Keefe Brasselle in *The Eddie Cantor Story* (US 53)

Lon Chaney by James Cagney in *The Man of a Thousand Faces* (US 57)

Lon Chaney Jr by Roger Smith in *The Man of a Thousand Faces* (US 57)

Charlie Chaplin by Leslie Henson in *The Real Thing at Last* (GB 16); by Richard Bell in

Perhaps the only two leading ladies ever to have upstaged Marilyn Monroe, Tony Curtis and Jack Lemmon were her co-stars in **Some Like it Hot**.

The King of Comedy Visits China (China 22)

Montgomery Clift by Bill Vint in *Marilyn the Untold Story* (US 80)–TVM

Joan Crawford by Faye Dunaway in *Mommie Dearest* (US 81)

Tony Curtis by Bruce Neckels in *Marilyn the Untold Story* (US 80)–TVM

Marlene Dietrich by Shirley Temple in *The Incomparable More Legs Sweetnik* (US 32); by Margit Carstensen in *Adolf and Marlene* (W. Ger 77)

Marie Dressler by Hermione Baddeley in *Harlow* (US 65)

Frances Farmer by Jessica Lange in *Frances* (US 82); by Sheila McLaughlin in *Committed* (US 84)

W. C. Fields by Bill Oberlin in *Train Ride to Hollywood* (US 75); by Rod Steiger in *W. C. Fields and Me* (US 76)

Clark Gable by James Brolin in *Gable and Lombard* (US 76); by Larry Pennell in *Marilyn the Untold Story* (US 80)–TVM

Carlos Gardel by Gregorio Manzur in *Tangos–Gardel's Exile* (Fr/Arg 85)

☆ **Cary Grant** by John Gavin in *Sophia Loren–Her Own Story* (US 80)–TVM

Corinne Griffith by 6-year-old Linda Bruhl in *Papa's Delicate Condition* (US 63)

Oliver Hardy by John 'Red' Fox in *Harlow* (US 65)

Jean Harlow by Carroll Baker in *Harlow* (US 65); by Carol Lynley in *Harlow* (US 65)–different movie; and by drag artiste Mario Montez in *Harlot* (US 65)

June Havoc by Suzanne Capito and Ann Jilliann in *Gypsy* (US 62)

Al Jolson by Larry Parks in *The Jolson Story* (US 46) and *Jolson Sings Again* (US 49)

Annette Kellerman by Esther Williams in *Million Dollar Mermaid* (US 53)

Hedy Lamarr by drag artiste Mario Montez in *Hedy (The Fourteen Year Old Girl)* (US 76)

Stan Laurel by Jim Plunkett in *Harlow* (US 65)

Jack Lemmon by Brad Blaisdell in *Marilyn the Untold Story* (US 80)–TVM

Bruce Lee by Hsaio Lung in *The Bruce Lee Story* (US 74); by Li Msiu Hsien in *Bruce Lee and I* (HK 76)

Vivien Leigh by Morgan Brittany in *Gable and Lombard* (US 76)

Carole Lombard by Jill Clayburgh in *Gable and Lombard* (US 76)

A. E. Matthews by Roland Culver in *No Longer Alone* (GB 78)

Marilyn Monroe by Misty Rowe in *Goodbye, Norma Jean* (Aus/US 76); by Catherine Hicks in *Marilyn the Untold Story* (US 80)–TVM; and by Theresa Russell in *Insignificance* (GB 85)

Renate Muller by Ruth Leuwerik in *Liebling der Götter* (W. Ger 60)

Nazimova by Leslie Caron in *Valentino* (GB 77)

Laurence Olivier by Anthony Gordon in *Marilyn the Untold Story* (US 80)–TVM

George Raft by Ray Danton in *The George Raft Story* (US 61)

Will Rogers by A. A. Trimble in *The Great Ziegfeld* (US 36); by Will Rogers Jr in *The Story of Will Rogers* (US 50) and *The Eddie Cantor Story* (US 53)

*Jessica Lange as Frances Farmer in **Frances** (US 82).*

The real Frances Farmer. A deeply disturbed woman, she served time in gaol and was eventually lobotomised and committed to an asylum.

Lana Turner by drag artiste Mario Montez in *More Milk, Yvette* (US 66)

Rudolph Valentino by Anthony Dexter in *Valentino* (US 51); by Rudolf Nureyev in *Valentino* (GB 77); by Matt Collins in *The World's Greatest Lover* (US 77); and by Martin Snaric in *The Last Remake of Beau Geste* (US 77)

Richard Widmark by László Szabó in *Made in USA* (Fr 67).

HOLLYWOOD HOWLERS

BLUNDERS

Movie bloopers are most common in historical films, because usually the people who make them haven't studied a lot of history. Less usual is making a boo-boo in the title, but that happens too. Both these categories have lists of their own, following this one, which is devoted to the general all-purpose cock-up.

☆ In Michael Powell's *The Edge of the World* (GB 37), Belle Crystal plays a barefoot Scottish lassie on the island of Foula. Well, sometimes barefoot. She is seen running down a hillside to the shore with nothing on her pretty feet. She runs up it again in shoes, without having paused to put them on, and she is definitely still shod when she reaches the top. Without removing her shoes, she sets off for the shore again and arrives on naked feet.

☆ During Judy Garland's performance of The Trolley Song in *Meet Me in St Louis* (US 44) a clearly audible voice on the soundtrack calls out 'Hi, Judy!'– evidently a friend who had just come on set and thought the star was only rehearsing.

☆ Washington's Lincoln Memorial is located in New York in the German version of *Uncle Tom's Cabin* (W. Ger 65).

☆ The camera is reflected in a mirror in the Robert De Niro–Meryl Streep movie *Falling in Love* (US 85).

☆ All the cars seen in the London street scenes in the Danny Kaye movie *Knock on Wood* (US 54) are left-hand drive. In another Danny Kaye film, *Merry Andrew* (US 58), a London bus is progressing along the right-hand side of the road.

☆ As the students rush up the back stairs of Covent Garden Opera House to the gods in *The Red Shoes* (US 48), the wall distinctly wobbles as only canvas stretched on a wooden frame can wobble.

☆ A character in *Man About the House* (GB 74) hails a taxi outside what is clearly Thames Television Studios and asks the driver to take him to Thames TV. On arrival he is seen getting out at exactly the spot at which he got in.

☆ The hero's flat in Portman Square in *Twenty-Three Paces to Baker Street* (US 56) has a balcony overlooking the Thames. Portman Square is over two miles away from London's river.

☆ MGM/UA had to send a letter of apology to Alaskan State Senator Jan Falks after they had publicised *Red Dawn* (US 84) with the declaration: 'In our time, no foreign army has ever occupied American soil. Until now." Someone in MGM/UA marketing was too young to remember the Japanese occupation of the Aleutians in World War II. The slogan continued to run, however, the distributors defending it with the somewhat specious argument that 'in our time' did not necessarily include the war.

☆ Mike Hammer (Ralph Meeker) in **Kiss Me Deadly** (US 55) goes up to a street kiosk, buys some popcorn, and walks away eating it, a sequence lasting a few seconds. The clock in the background shows 2.10 pm when he approaches the kiosk, 2.15 pm as he buys the popcorn, and 2.20 pm as he departs.

☆ Set in Vienna, **Wonder Child** (GB/Austria 51) was made with Austrian actors speaking English. For Austrian and German release the producers made the curious decision to have the film dubbed not by the original actors, but by Germans speaking in Berlin accents. The picture's reception in Vienna was less than favourable.

☆ A corpse in a battle scene in **Son of Ali Baba** (US 52) moves its arm just as someone is about to step on it.

☆ A scene in a bar in **The In-Laws** (US 79) with Peter Falk sitting at the counter next to a cabbie has the pair switching places in the cutaway shots.

☆ **Crash Landing** (US 58) begins at Lisbon Airport. The planes seen in the background are clearly marked 'Western Air Lines', a US domestic carrier.

☆ In Tony Richardson's film of Nabokov's **Laughter in the Dark** (GB 69), Nicol Williamson enters the Curzon Cinema but finds himself in the auditorium of the National Film Theatre.

☆ The credits of the Indian film **Shiraz** (India 28) headed the list of players with the word 'Caste'.

☆ In **The Private Life of Sherlock Holmes** (GB 70), Holmes refers to a newspaper he has spied at the bottom of a birdcage as the *Inverness Courier*. The infallible detective is wrong. It is the *Inverness Times*.

☆ The gung-ho flagwagger **The Marines Are Here** (US 38) showed a gallant marine scaling a very high wall by climbing on the shoulders of his buddy. The next scene shows him dropping to the ground on the other side–closely followed by his buddy, who has apparently scaled the wall unassisted.

☆ In **Jaws** (US 75), when the citizens of Amity celebrate 4 July, there are no leaves on the trees. (The scene was shot in May.)

☆ The title cards of silent western **Hands Across the Border** (US 26) refer several times to wonder horse Silver King as 'she'. As the name suggests, Silver King was a stallion.

☆ In **The Barbarian and the Geisha** (US 58) John Wayne absentmindedly addresses Sam Jaffe, playing a character called Henry Heuken, as Sam instead of Henry.

☆ In an old English country house scene in **Great Impersonation** (US 35), Edmund Lowe is seen going to bed by candlelight. When he is woken during the night, there is an electric light switch handy.

☆ Kathleen Turner is wearing canvas slip-ons as she leaps from a roof-top onto a train in **The Jewel of the Nile** (US 86). As she stumbles and falls, clinging to the side of the train, she is wearing leather open-work sandals; but on being rescued, she struggles to her feet and the sandals have been replaced once more by the canvas slip-ons.

ANACHRONISMS

☆ Television aerials are visible on the roofs of Victorian London in **The Wrong Box** (GB 66).

☆ As Scarlett leaves the hospital in Atlanta in **Gone With the Wind** (US 39) she runs past a street lamp lit by electricity.

☆ A steam locomotive is seen drawing a train out of Grand Central in **Midnight Limited** (US 40), a story set in the present. All locos in and out of Grand Central were electric by 1940.

☆ The heroine of **Adalen 31** (Swe 69), set in 1931, removes her clothes in one scene and reveals bikini marks.

☆ Dynamite is exploded in **Tap Roots** (US 48), set in 1860. Dynamite was invented in 1867.

☆ The action of **The Sound of Music** (US 65) is set in the 1930s, yet in one scene an orange box can be discerned stamped 'Produce of Israel'.

☆ Playing a racketeer, Edward G. Robinson gets sent to Alcatraz in 1927 in **The Last Gangster** (US 37). Alcatraz did not become a penal institution until 1934.

☆ In **Slumber Party '57** (US 77) a girl is seen reading *Lolita* a year before the novel was published.

☆ A British Rail sign can be seen in the World War II drama **The Cockleshell Heroes** (GB 55).

British Rail was established in 1948.

☆ The Good King in **Saint Wenceslas** (Cz 29) wore a wristwatch.

☆ **Sutter's Gold** (US 36) showed New Yorkers of the 1840s wearing pyjamas.

☆ Anachronisms are usually visual or in the dialogue. In **The Draughtsman's Contract** (GB

*Note the orange box stamped 'Produce of Israel'. **The Sound of Music** took place more than a decade before the founding of the State of Israel.*

83) it is a background noise that dispels, at least for ornithologists, the illusion of the film's 17th-century setting. The gentle cooing of a collared dove is not a sound that would have fallen on Jacobean ears. The species was unknown in Britain until 1955.

☆ While only an expert would have been conscious of the preceding anachronism, most audiences would have been fully aware that the word 'gay', used throughout the dialogue of **Victor/Victoria** (GB 82), did not mean homosexual in the 1930s.

☆ The prehistoric man thawed back to life in **Return of the Apeman** (US 44) is wearing cotton underwear underneath his animal skins.

☆ Laird Cregar dies beneath Tower Bridge in **The Lodger** (US 44), set in 1888. Tower Bridge was built in 1894.

☆ President Lincoln admits California into the Union in 1847 in **Der Kaiser von Kalifornien** (Ger 36). In fact James Polk was President at the time; Lincoln did not become President until 14 years later.

☆ Richard Harris played his role of King Arthur in **Camelot** (US 67) with a piece of Elastoplast visible on his neck.

☆ Tyre tracks are clearly apparent on the stagecoach route in **Stagecoach** (US 66).

☆ Trains in Britain often run late, but the blue and yellow BR Inter-City train which flashes by in **Quadrophenia** (GB 79)–set in 1964–is 14 years early.

☆ In the Agatha Christie whodunnit **Eye of the Needle** (GB 82), set in 1938, the dollar conversion rate is quoted at its 1981 level.

☆ In a scene set in 1945 in **The Godfather** (US 72) there is an American flag with 50 stars. There were 48 states in the Union at that date.

MISLEADING TITLES

☆**Tracked by the Police** (US 27) was a Rin Tin Tin vehicle whose title was decided by Warner's before the script was written. In fact Rin Tin Tin was the tracker, with never a policeman in sight.

☆ **Thirteen Women** (US 32), about a half-cast girl revenging the racial slights of her childhood by murdering each of her now adult tormentors, has only ten women in it. **Seven Women from Hell** (US 61) is about six women.

☆ Similarly Mikhail Romm's **The Thirteen** (USSR 36) was so titled because it was supposed to be about a desert patrol of 13 soldiers. Anyone in the audience who bothered to count would have noticed there were only twelve soldiers. **Her Twelve Men** (US 54), by contrast, had Greer Garson as a schoolteacher in charge of a class of thirteen pupils.

☆ **The Black Cat** (US 34) had nothing to do with the Poe story of the same name (despite a credit to Poe) and nothing to do with a black cat other than the fact a cat crept in and out of a few scenes, irrelevantly, to justify the title.

☆ **Eine Nacht in London** (Ger/GB 34) was released in Britain as One Knight in London.

☆ **Exiled to Shanghai** (US 37)

Abbott and Costello Go to Mars–or is it Venus? In fact, do they ever leave Earth?

☆ **South of Rio** (US 49) takes place well north of it.

☆ The assault in **Assault on Precinct 13** (US 76) is, in fact, on Precinct 9.

☆ **The Amorous Prawn** (GB 62) was about a general's wife who opens their official home in the Highlands to American paying guests. In America the title was changed to *The Playgirl and the War Minister*, despite the fact there was no playgirl and no War Minister in the film–the date explains the choice, as 1962 was the height of the Profumo affair.

☆ **Big Hand for a Little Lady** (US 66) was released in Britain as *Big Deal at Dodge City*. Whoever thought this up had not seen the picture. It was set in Laredo.

☆ **Krakatoa, East of Java** (US 68) wasn't. Krakatoa was 200 miles *west* of Java.

was not about anyone being exiled and the story did not play in Shanghai.

☆ **Roundup Time in Texas** (US 37) is about roundup time on the South African veldt.

☆ **Adventures in Iraq** (US 43) was set in Syria.

☆ **The Courage of Lassie** (US 46) did not have Lassie in it. Elizabeth Taylor's dog in the film was called Bill.

☆ In **Abbott and Costello Meet the Killer, Boris Karloff** (US 48), Boris Karloff is not the killer. In **Abbott and Costello Go to Mars** (US 53) they don't. They go to Venus.

CLASHES

The simultaneous release of Gregory Ratoff's **Oscar Wilde** (GB 60), with Robert Morley, and Ken Hughes' **The Trials of Oscar Wilde** (GB 60), with Peter Finch, drew attention to a phenomenon which has been commoner in the history of movies than is generally realised. As early as 1912 the first feature film made in Britain and the first feature film made in America were rival versions of **Oliver Twist** and that same year no less than three different productions of **The Last Days of Pompeii** were made in Italy. Here are some of the more notable examples of movie 'clashes'.

☆ Two Russian adaptations of

War and Peace were actually released on the same day, 13 February 1915, and the same thing happened the next year in America when both the Francis X. Bushman-Beverly Bayne and Harry Hilliard-Theda Bara versions of *Romeo and Juliet* were premiered on 22 October 1916.

☆ As many as eight biopics of the rascally monk Rasputin were made in 1917, four in Russia, three in the USA and one in Germany.

☆ In 1934 Marlene Dietrich's bravura performance in and as *The Scarlet Empress* (US 34) eclipsed Elizabeth Bergner's less vibrant interpretation of *Catherine the Great* (GB 34).

☆ The following year there was another clash of costume dramas with Josef von Sternberg's American version of *Crime and Punishment*, starring Peter Lorre, and Pierre Chanal's French production with Pierre Blanchar.

☆ America and France clashed again in 1936 when audiences could choose between the Hollywood biopic *Louis Pasteur* with Paul Muni or the more authentic portrayal of the great scientist by Sacha Guitry in the version titled simply *Pasteur*.

☆ Two feature-length cartoon versions of *Cinderella* appeared in 1950, one from Walt Disney in America, the other from Estela Film in Spain.

☆ Disney had competition again the following year when his cartoon version of *Alice in Wonderland* was on release at the same time as Lou Bunin's puppet and live-action version with Carol Marsh as Alice.

☆ Twin films about the July plot to kill Hitler, one titled *The 20th July*, the other *It Happened on 20th July*, were released in Germany on successive days in 1955.

☆ Mario Lanza was not the only actor to play *The Great Caruso* in 1951. Ermanno Randi starred in a rival Italian biopic, titled *Enrico Caruso, Legend of a Voice*.

☆ When the Italian director Franco Zeffirelli made a British production of *Romeo and Juliet* in 1968 with Leonard Whiting and Olivia Hussey, an Italian production of the great love story was made by Ricardo Freda with Gerald Meynier and Rosemarie Dexter. This version was brought to London for dubbing, but hoping to penetrate the lucrative American market, Signor Freda chose to have it done in that most unromantic of accents, Brooklynese!

☆ Another clash of classics–this time with some real competition at the box office–came in 1975 with the simultaneous release of Patrick Garland's *A Doll's House*, with Claire Bloom as Nora, and Joseph Losey's *A Doll's House* with Jane Fonda. Both these were British productions, but there was also a German version the same year, directed by Rainer Werner Fassbinder and starring Margit Carstensen.

☆ Two biopics titled *Harlow* (US 65), one with Carroll Baker as the thirties star, the other with Carol Lynley, were joined by a third from the Andy Warhol stable titled *Harlot* (US 65). In this rather unconventional version, the Blonde Venus was portrayed by Mario Montez in drag.

☆ The well-loved children's classic *The Little Mermaid* appeared in three different versions in 1976–a Czech production, a Finnish production, and a USSR-Bulgarian co-production.

☆ **The Elephant Man** (GB 80), with John Hurt, was one of the box office successes of 1980, but not many people were aware of the Canadian version produced the same year.

☆ Released within twelve months of each other, if not the same year, were the three treatments of the Entebbe Raid story, **Victory at Entebbe** (US 76), **Raid on Entebbe** (US 76), and the most accurate version of the events, **Operation Thunderbolt** (Isr 77).

☆ Opera buffs were confronted with no less than seven versions of **Carmen** in 1984, albeit three of them from the same director. Peter Brook filmed his French stage production with three different casts, the title role being taken by Helene Delavault, Zehavá Gal and Eva Saurova. Julia Migenes-Johnson took the part in Fracesco Rossi's Italian-French co-production, Anne-Marie Mühle in Roland Sterner's Swedish production, Stefania Toczyska in Mate Rabinovski's French production and Laura del Sol in Carlos Saura's Spanish production. An eighth version of Carmen, based on Merimée's story rather than Bizet's opera, was **Carmen Nue** with Pamela Prati in the title role.

☆ **Wills and Burke** (Aus 85) was released a week before **Burke and Wills** (Aus 85). The latter is a straight presentation of the story of Australia's most celebrated explorers, the former a parody. Uniquely in a clash situation there were two actors, Peter Collingwood and Chris Haywood, who appeared in both versions. (Any listing of either actor's credits is going to read like a mistake.)

PLAY IT AGAIN, SAM

REMAKES

These are the twenty stories which have been told most often on screen. The totals given include modern versions and parodies, but not television dramas. The order differs from that of the remakes list in the 2nd edition of *The Guinness Book of Film Facts*

and *Feats*, partly because of recent remakes but also because of new research that has revealed further remakes of the past. In ascending order:

18 A Christmas Carol (Dickens)

18 Anna Karenina (Tolstoy)

19 Julius Caesar (Shakespeare)

19 The Tell-Tale Heart (Poe)

20 A Midsummer Night's Dream (Shakespeare)

21 Oliver Twist (Dickens)

23 Resurrection (Tolstoy)

25 Harischandra (Hindu epic)

28 Les Misérables (Hugo)

29 The Three Musketeers (Dumas père)

29 Macbeth (Shakespeare)

35 Don Quixote (Cervantes)

36 La Dame aux Camelias (Dumas fils)

40 Robinson Crusoe (Defoe)

42 Romeo and Juliet (Shakespeare)

46 Doctor Jekyll and Mr Hyde (Stevenson)

48 Faust (Marlowe, Goethe and Gunod's opera)

56 Carmen (Merimée and Bizet's opera)

60 Hamlet (Shakespeare)

81 Cinderella (traditional)

COMEBACKS

Sometimes a star of yesteryear re-emerges after a long absence from the screen. Here are those who made their comeback at least 15 years after their previous picture. The British record is held by the former child star Dorothy Batley, who made her screen debut aged 8 in 1910, left the screen when she was 17, and made a comeback 31 years later as a middle aged matron. The Hollywood record is held by the inimitable Mae West with a comeback after 35 years.

☆ **Dorothy Batley** (31 years)
The Sins of Youth (GB 19)

The Angel with the Trumpet (GB 50)

☆ **Betty Bronson** (26 years)
The Yodellin' Kid from Pine Ridge (US 37)
The Naked Kiss (US 63)

☆ **George Burns** (26 years)
Honolulu (US 39)
The Sunshine Boys (US 75)

☆ **James Cagney** (20 years)
One Two Three (US 61)
Ragtime (US 81)

☆ **Frances Farmer** (16 years)
Son of Fury (US 42)
The Party Crashers (US 58)

☆ **Alice Faye** (17 years)
Fallen Angel (US 45)
State Fair (US 62)

☆ **Janet Gaynor** (19 years)
The Young in Heart (US 38)
Bernardine (US 57)

☆ **Madge Kennedy** (26 years)
Oh Baby! (US 26)
The Marrying Kind (US 52)

☆ **Deborah Kerr** (16 years)
The Arrangement (US 69)
The Assam Garden (GB 85)

☆ **Piper Laurie** (15 years)
The Hustler (US 61)
Carrie (US 76)

☆ **Margaret Lockwood** (21 years)
Cast a Dark Shadow (GB 55)
The Slipper and the Rose (GB 76)

☆ **Ida Lupino** (16 years)
Strange Intruder (US 56)
Junior Bonner (US 72)

☆ **Pola Negri** (21 years)
Hi Diddle Diddle (US 43)
The Moon Spinners (US 64)

☆ **Roy Rogers** (24 years)
Son of Paleface (US 52)
Mackintosh and T.J. (US 76)–
NB: no horse

☆ **Ann Savage** (33 years)
The Woman They Almost

*Mae West left the screen in 1943 after **The Heat's On** and did not return until 35 years later in **Myra Breckenridge**.*

Lynched (US 53)
Captive Hearts (Can 86)

☆ **Lizabeth Scott** (15 years)
Quantrill's Raiders (US 58)
Pulp (US 73)

☆ **Dinah Sheridan** (17 years)
The Story of Gilbert and Sullivan (GB 53)
The Railway Children (GB 70)

☆ **Sylvia Sidney** (17 years)
Behind the High Wall (US 56)
Summer Wishes, Winter Dreams (US 73)

☆ **Gale Sondergaard** (20 years)
East Side, West Side (US 49)
Slaves (US 69)

☆ **Gloria Swanson** (18 years)
Nero's Mistress (It 56)
Airport 75 (US 74)

☆ **Mae West** (35 years)
The Heat's On (US 43)
Myra Breckenridge (US 78)

DOUBLE TAKES

One of the best accolades for an acting performance is to be asked to play the same role in the remake. Here are the few who have done so.

☆ **Florence Arliss** (Mrs George Arliss) as the Countess of Beaconsfield (Mrs Disraeli) in *Disraeli* (US 21) and (US 30)

☆ **George Arliss** in the title role of *Disraeli* (US 21) and (US 30)

☆ **George Arliss** as the Rajah of Rukh in *The Green Goddess* (US 23) and (US 30)

☆ **John Barrymore** as Capt Ahab in *The Sea Beast* (US 26) and *Moby Dick* (US 30)

☆ **Lon Chaney** as Echo the Ventriloquist in *The Unholy Three* (US 25) and (US 30)

☆ **Finlay Currie** as Alastair McBain in ***Rome Express*** (GB 33) and ***Sleeping Car to Trieste*** (GB 48)

☆ **Douglas Dumbrille** as Eddie Morgan in ***Broadway Bill*** (US 34) and ***Riding High*** (US 50)–see also Raymond Walburn

☆ **W. C. Fields** as Prof Eustace McGargle in ***Sally of the Sawdust*** (US 25) and ***Poppy*** (US 36)

☆ **Margarita Fischer** as Topsy in ***Uncle Tom's Cabin*** (US 13) and (US 27)

☆ **Alan Hale** as Little John in ***Robin Hood*** (US 22), ***The Adventures of Robin Hood*** (US 38) and ***The Rogues of Sherwood Forest*** (US 50)

☆ **Sir Seymour Hicks** in the title role of ***Scrooge*** (GB 13) and (GB 35)

☆ **Clark Gable** as rubber planter Dennis Carson in ***Red Dust*** (US 32) and African big game hunter Victor Marswell in ***Mogambo*** (US 53)
NB same character under different names

☆ **Greta Garbo** as Anna in ***Love*** (US 27) and ***Anna Karenina*** (US 35)

☆ **Edmund Gwenn** as Hornblower in ***The Skin Game*** (US 20) and (US 31)

☆ **Kazuo Hasegawa** in double role of the actor and the thief in ***The Revenge of Yukino-Jo*** (Jap 35) and (Jap 63)

☆ **Eileen Herlie** as Queen Gertrude in ***Hamlet*** (GB 48) and (US 64)

☆ **Edward Everett Horton** as Nick Potter in ***Holiday*** (US 30) and (US 38)

☆ **Tito Lusiardo** as Pascual in

The Day You Love Me (US 35) and (Arg 69)
NB record for longest interval between original and remake

☆ **Frank McHugh** as the drunken thief Skippy in ***One Way Passage*** (US 32) and ***Till we Meet Again*** (US 39)

☆ **George Martin** as Chris Christopherson in ***Anna Christie*** (US 23) and (US 30)

☆ **Ivor Novello** as Angeloff in ***The Lodger*** (GB 26) and ***The Phantom Fiend*** (GB 33)

☆ **Elizabeth Patterson** as Mrs Ward in ***Guilty as Hell*** (US 32) and ***Night Club Scandal*** (US 37)

☆ **Mary Pickford** in the title role of ***Tess of the Storm Country*** (US 14) and (US 22)

☆ **ZaSu Pitts** as the maid Pauline in ***No, No, Nanette*** (US 30) and (US 40)

☆ **Anthony Quinn** in ***Zorba the Greek*** (GB 64) and ***Zorba the Musical*** (US 87)

☆ **George Robey** as Sancho Panza in ***Don Quixote*** (GB 23) and (GB 33)

☆ **Athene Seyler** as the aunt in ***Quiet Wedding*** (GB 41) and ***Happy Is the Bride*** (GB 58)

☆ **Otis Skinner** as Hajj in ***Kismet*** (US 20) and (US 30)

☆ **Francis L. Sullivan** as Jaggers in ***Great Expectations*** (US 35) and (GB 47)

☆ **Raymond Walburn** as con man Col Pettigrew in ***Broadway Bill*** (US 34) and ***Riding High*** (US 50)

☆ **Harry B. Walthall** as Hester's husband in ***The Scarlet Letter*** (US 26) and (US 34)

☆ **H. B. Warner** as Sorrell in ***Sorrell and Son*** (US 27) and (GB 34).

HOLLYWOOD AND SPORT

THE LEAGUE TABLE

Hollywood had made a total of 703 feature films with a sports background up to the end of 1985. The most popular sport as a subject for screen drama is boxing, with just under 25% of the total, followed by horse racing with 16.6% and motor racing with 14.5%. The number of films devoted to each sport in each decade is listed below, with the various sports in rank order according to their individual totals. Only films about competitive sport have been included, so few of the films of Esther Williams, for example, have been counted under swimming.

	1910 –19	1920 –29	1930 –39	1940 –49	1950 –59	1960 –69	1970 –79	1980 –85	TOTAL
Boxing	–	61	39	29	28	4	11	5	177
Horse Racing	1	32	44	21	11	5	3	–	117
American Football	2	23	38	14	10	5	8	2	102
Motor Racing	2	23	20	3	10	16	8	–	82
Baseball	5	9	7	7	13	1	7	4	53
Athletics	–	8	2	–	3	3	8	4	28
Basketball	–	2	2	–	3	2	12	3	24
Golf	–	1	4	–	3	4	1	1	14
Wrestling	–	–	2	1	–	–	7	4	14
Motor Cycle Racing	–	2	1	–	1	3	6	–	13
Polo	–	6	4	–	–	–	–	–	10
Speedboat Racing	–	1	6	–	–	–	2	–	9
Rowing	–	5	4	–	–	–	–	–	9
Skiing	–	–	1	1	–	2	2	3	9
Ice Hockey	–	–	3	1	1	–	1	–	6
Tennis	–	1	1	–	1	–	3	–	6
Swimming	–	2	–	–	1	–	1	1	5
Cycle Racing	–	–	1	–	–	–	1	2	4
Roller Skating	–	–	–	–	–	–	4	–	4
Ice Skating	–	–	1	–	–	–	1	–	2
Pool	–	–	–	–	–	–	1	–	1
Skateboarding	–	–	–	–	–	–	2	–	2
Soccer	–	–	–	–	–	–	–	2	2
Yacht Racing	–	–	1	–	–	1	–	–	2
Angling	–	–	–	–	–	1	–	–	1
Bowling	–	–	–	–	–	1	–	–	1
Cockfighting	–	–	–	–	–	1	–	–	1
Dog Racing	–	–	1	–	–	–	–	–	1
Fencing	–	1	–	–	–	–	–	–	1
Gymnastics	–	–	–	–	–	–	–	1	1
Ice Yachting	–	1	–	–	–	–	–	–	1
Showjumping	–	–	–	–	–	1	–	–	1
Weightlifting	–	–	–	–	–	–	1	–	1

OLYMPIC MOVIES

Considering the drama as well as the popular appeal of the Olympics, it is perhaps surprising that they are not more often used as the setting for movies. These are the ones that have been made.

Olympic Honeymoon (GB 36) A light-hearted romp in which Claude Hulbert, as an estranged honeymooner, is mistaken for an ice hockey champion and helps Britain win the gold at the Winter Olympics. (The British team did in fact win in 1936.)

Charlie Chan at the Olympics (US 37) Hokum about spies being pursued by the inscrutable Chinese detective to Berlin, where 'No 1 Son' is a member of the US swimming team competing at the Olympics.

Jim Thorpe–All-American (US 51) Biopic with Burt Lancaster as the Oklahoma Indian who won the decathlon and pentathlon events at Stockholm in 1912, but was forced to return his medals when it was found he had played a few games of semi-pro baseball for coffee-and-cake money.

The Bob Mathias Story (US 54) Autobiopic with Bob Mathias, who won the decathlon twice, at London in 1948 and Helsinki in 1952, playing himself and his wife Melba playing herself.

Geordie (GB 55) Bill Travers as a weakly Scots lad who takes a body building course and wins the hammer throwing event at the Melbourne Olympics.

It Happened in Athens (US 62) Trax Cotton as untrained Greek shepherd lad winning the marathon at the first modern Olympics at Athens in 1896.

Walk, Don't Run (US 66) Cary Grant, in his last film appearance, as one of an ill-assorted group who wind up living in Samantha Eggar's flat during the Tokyo Olympics due to shortage of accommodation.

The Games (GB 70) Story of four marathon runners from different countries competing at Rome Olympics. Starring Ryan O'Neal and Michael Crawford.

International Velvet (GB 78) Tatum O'Neal as niece of the Velvet played by Elizabeth Taylor as a child in *National Velvet*. Orphan comes to Britain from US,

*Burt Lancaster as tragic Red Indian Olympic medallist Jim Thorpe in **Jim Thorpe–All American**.*

has difficulty settling down, takes to show-jumping at prompting of Velvet (Nanette Newman), and eventually triumphs in Olympics.

Running (Can 79) Michael Douglas as American marathon runner overcoming injury at the Montreal Olympics. (It is typical of Canadian films that the hero is American rather than Canadian.)

Dawn (Aus 79) Bronwyn Mackay-Payne plays the big Aussie swimmer Dawn Fraser who won three golds at Melbourne '56, Rome '60 and Tokyo '64 and was then banned for ten years for stealing a flag at the Tokyo Games.

Goldengirl (US 79) Susan Anton as lissom blonde runner brainwashed and physically coerced by unscrupulous coach and adoptive father into winning three golds at the 1980 Moscow Olympics. (As the US did not compete, all the agony would have been for nothing.)

Chariots of Fire (GB 81) David Puttnam's quadruple Oscar winner about Jewish athlete, Harold Abrahams (Ben Cross), who provoked controversy by hiring a professional coach to train him for the 1924 Paris Olympics, and Eric Liddel (Ian Charleson), the Scottish sprinter who refused to race on the Sabbath.

Running Brave (Can 83) Biopic of Sioux Indian Robby Benson, winner of the 10,000 metres at the 1964 Tokyo Games.

Nadia (US 84) Leslie Weiner and Johann (yes, it is a girl's name) Carlo as the younger and older Nadia Comaneci, elf-like Romanian who took the triple gold for gymnastics at the 1976 Montreal Olympics.

SPORTING CHANCE

Sportsmen dream of being movie stars just like the rest of us. Some of them have had a crack at it. A few have played fictitious characters, but those listed below appeared as themselves.

Muhammed Ali, heavyweight boxing champion, in ***The Greatest*** (US 77)

Vijay Amritraj, Indian tennis champion, in ***Octopussy*** (GB 83)

Mario Andretti, motor racing driver, in ***Speed Fever*** (It 78)

Max Baer, heavyweight boxing champion, in ***The Prizefighter and the Lady*** (US 33)

Yogi Berra, baseball star, in ***That Touch of Mink*** (US 62)

Danny Blanchflower, soccer star, in ***Those Glory, Glory Days*** (GB 83)

Bjorn Borg, tennis champion, in ***Racquet*** (US 79)

Ty Cobb, baseball star, in ***Somewhere in Georgia*** (US 17)

Dennis Compton, cricketer, in ***The Final Test*** (GB 53)

Jack Dempsey, heavyweight boxing champion, in ***Off Limits*** (US 53)

Joe Frazier, heavyweight boxing champion, in ***Rocky*** (US 77)

Graham Hill, motor racing driver, in ***The Fast Lady*** (GB 62)

Ben Hogan, golfer, in ***The Caddy*** (US 53)

James Hunt, motor racing driver, in ***Speed Fever*** (It 78)

Jack Johnson, heavyweight boxing champion, in ***As the World Rolls On*** (US 21)

Suzanne Lenglen, tennis champion, in ***Things Are***

Looking Up (GB 35)

Joe Louis, heavyweight boxing champion, in *The Spirit of Youth* (US 37)

Jem Mace, bare knuckle prizefighter, in *There's Life In the Old Dog Yet* (GB 08)

John McEnroe, tennis champion, in *Players* (US 79)

Bob Mathias, twice winner of Olympic decathlon, in *The Bob Mathias Story* (US 54)

Gussie Moran, tennis champion, in *Pat and Mike* (US 52)

Stirling Moss, motor racing driver, in *The Beauty Contest* (GB 64)

Arnold Palmer, golfer, in *Call Me Bwana* (US 63)

Pele, Brazilian soccer star, in *Young Giants* (US 83)

Sir Gordon Richards, champion jockey, in *The Rainbow Jacket* (GB 54)

Jackie Robinson, first black to play major league baseball, in *The Jackie Robinson Story* (US 50)

Sugar Ray Robinson, heavyweight boxing champion, in *Paper Lion* (US 68)

Barry Sheene, world motor cycle racing champion, in *Space Riders* (GB 85)

O. J. Simpson, gridiron football star, in *The Klansman* (US 74)

Guillermo Vilas, tennis player, in *Players* (US 79).

HOLY ORDERS

GOD SLOT

A lot of actors think they're God, but few have actually been cast in the role. Here are those who have played God on screen.

Rex Ingram in *Green Pastures* (US 36)

Lionel Barrymore in *A Guy Named Joe* (US 43)

Fernandel in *The Devil and the Ten Commandments* (Fr/It 62)

Donald Sutherland in *Johnny Got His Gun* (US 71)

George Burns in *Oh, God!* (US 77)

George Burns in *Oh, God! Book II* (US 80)

Richard Pryor in *In God We Trust* (US 80)

Allan Love in *The Apple* (US 80)

Ralph Richardson in *Time Bandits* (GB 81)

Renzo Rinaldi in *Council of Love* (W. Ger 82)

Robert Morley in *Second Time Lucky* (NZ/Aus 84)

George Burns in *Oh, God! You Devil* (US 84)

Ferdy Mayne in *Night Train to Terror* (US 85).

ADAM AND EVE

Movie goers confronted with any filmic versions of Genesis should spare a glance at Adam's midriff. If, as in John Huston's *The Bible* (US 66), he has a navel–well, he shouldn't, should he?

Opportunities to check this out are limited, as there have only been 15 movies depicting Adam and Eve. The list below does not include the four films for which no credits have been traced: *The Birth of a Race* (US 19); *The Old Testament* (It 22); *A Night in Hell* (Iran 58); and *Angels and Cherubs* (Mex 72).

1 **Theodore Kosloff** in *The Tree of Knowledge* (US 20). *NB* Eve does not appear.

2 **George O'Brien** and **Olive Burden** in *Fig Leaves* (US 26).

3 **Rex Ingram** and **Myrtle Anderson** in *Green Pastures* (US 36).
NB Adam and Eve are both black.

4 **Bobby Todd** and **Bettina Moissi** in *The Apple Fell* (W. Ger 49).

5 **Macario** and **Isa Barzizza** in *Adam and Eve* (It 49).

6 **Carlos Baena** and **Christiane Martell** in *Adam and Eve* (Mex 56).

7 **Marty Milner** and **Mamie Van Doren** in *The Private Lives of Adam and Eve* (US 61).

8 **Michael Parks** and **Ulla Bergyrd** in *The Bible* (US/It 66).

9 **Bo White** and **Caprice Couselle** in *Bible* (US 74).

10 **Péter Bocsor** and **Julia Mérö** in *Annunciation* (Hun 84). *NB* all-child cast.

11 **Roger Wilson** and **Diane Franklin** in *Second Time Lucky* (NZ/Aus 84).

GHOSTS

Alec B. Francis in *The Return of Peter Grimm* (US 26)

Morton Selten in *The Ghost Goes West* (GB 36)

Constance Bennett in *Topper* (US 37)

Constance Bennett in *Topper*

*It's not only spooky old country mansions that are haunted–art deco apartments can be too, as the presence of a ghostly Constance Bennett testifies in **Topper**.*

Takes a Trip (US 39)

Lilli Palmer in *Thunder Rock* (GB 42)

Charles Laughton in *The Canterville Ghost* (US 44)

Cecil Kellaway and **Veronica Lake** in *I Married a Witch* (US 42)

Jack Oakie in *That's The Spirit* (US 45)

Kay Hammond in *Blithe Spirit* (GB 45)

Lou Costello in *The Time of Their Lives* (US 46)

Frank Morgan in *The Cockeyed Miracle* (US 46)

Rex Harrison in *The Ghost and Mrs Muir* (US 47)

Robert Morley and **Felix Aylmer** in *The Ghosts of Berkeley Square* (GB 47)

Alexander Archdale in *House of Darkness* (GB 48)

Jennifer Jones in *Portrait of Jennie* (US 48)

Jacques Tati in *Sylvie and the Phantom* (Fr 50)

James Mason in *Pandora and the Flying Dutchman* (GB 50)

Lloyd Corrigan in *Ghost Chasers* (US 51)

Joan Sterndale-Bennett in *No Haunt for a Gentleman* (GB 52)

Tod Slaughter in *A Ghost for Sale* (GB 52)

David Kossoff in *The Bespoke Overcoat* (GB 55)

Elvis Presley in *Love Me Tender* (US 56)

Clive Revill in *The Headless Ghost* (GB 59)

Peter Wyngarde and **Clydie Jessop** in *The Innocents* (GB 61)

Candace Hilligoss in *Carnival of Souls* (US 62)

Clive Revill did not allow playing the title role in **The Headless Ghost** *to go to his head.*

Susan Hart in *The Ghost in the Invisible Bikini* (US 66)

Lorne Gibson in *The Ghost Goes Gear* (GB 66)

Cass Daley in *The Spirit is Willing* (US 67)

Peter Ustinov in *Blackbeard's Ghost* (US 67)

Jimmy Edwards and **Graham Stark** in *A Ghost of a Chance* (GB 68)

David Niven in *The Extraordinary Seaman* (US 69)

Joseph Cotten in *Baron Blood* (It 72)

Jose Wilker in *Dona Flor and Her Two Husbands* (Br 77)

Vivian Stanshall in *Sir Henry at Rawlinson End* (GB 80)

Alice Krige in *Ghost Story* (US 81)

James Caan in *Kiss Me Goodbye* (US 82)

Glenn Close in *Maxie* (US 85)

HOLLYWOOD HATES

PUT DOWNS

Hollywood stars have a tendency to venerate each other, at least in public. It is reassuring to know that they do not always express such cloying sentiments in private.

Julie Andrews 'Working with her is like being hit over the head with a Valentine card.'–Christopher Plummer

Tallulah Bankhead 'A day away from Tallulah is like a month in the country.'–Howard Dietz

Diana Barrymore 'Diana is a horse's arse, quite a pretty one, but still a horse's arse'–her father, John Barrymore

John Barrymore 'It takes an earthquake to get Jack out of bed, a flood to make him wash, and the United States Army to put him to work'–his brother, Lionel Barrymore

Humphrey Bogart 'Bogey's a helluva nice guy until 11.30 pm. After that he thinks he's Bogart.'– Dave Chasen

Marlon Brando 'Most of the time he sounds like he has a mouth full of wet toilet paper.'–Rex Reed

Capucine Laurence Harvey to Capucine during filming of **Walk on the Wild Side** (US 62): 'If you were more of a woman, I would be more of a man. Kissing you is like kissing the side of a beer bottle.'

Maurice Chevalier 'A great artiste, but a small human being.'–Josephine Baker

Claudette Colbert Noel Coward to CC: 'I'd wring your neck, if you had one.'

Gary Cooper 'When he puts his arms around me, I feel like a horse.'–Clara Bow

'He's got a reputation as a great actor just by thinking hard about the next line.'–King Vidor

Joan Crawford 'The best time I ever had with Joan Crawford was when I pushed her down the stairs

According to Rex Reed, Brando sounds 'like he has a mouth full of wet toilet paper.'

in **Whatever Happened to Baby Jane**.'–Bette Davis

'There is not enough money in Hollywood to lure me into making another film with Joan Crawford.'–Sterling Hayden after co-starring with her in **Johnny Guitar** (US 54)

Bette Davis 'As much sex appeal as Slim Somerville.'–Carl Laemmle on BD in her youth

'I can't imagine any guy giving her a tumble.'–Carl Laemmle again

'Surely no one but a mother could have loved Bette Davis at the height of her career.'–Brian Ahearne

Doris Day 'I knew Doris Day before she was a virgin.'–Oscar Levant

'Doris Day is as wholesome as a bowl of cornflakes and at least as sexy.'–Dwight MacDonald

James Dean 'He was a hero to the people who saw him only as a little waif, when actually he was a pudding of hatred.'–Elia Kazan

Kirk Douglas '. . . boastful, egotistical, resentful of criticism–if anyone dare give it.'–Sheilah Graham

Nelson Eddy 'The ham of hams.'–Allan Dwan

Frances Farmer 'The nicest thing I can say about Frances Farmer is that she is unbearable.'–William Wyler

Errol Flynn 'A fifty-year trespass against good taste.'–Leslie Mallory

Clark Gable 'Clark Gable took the humour and sex from the characters he played.'–Joan Crawford

'. . . to tell the honest truth, he isn't such a helluva good lay'–his lover, subsequently his wife, Carole Lombard

Greta Garbo 'Boiled down to essentials, she is a plain mortal girl with large feet.'–Herbert Kretzmer

'The most inhibited person I've ever worked with.'–Ernst Lubitsch

'Making a film with Greta Garbo does not constitute an introduction.'–Robert Montgomery

Judy Garland 'Mother was the real-life Wicked Witch of the West.'–Liza Minnelli

Cary Grant 'An incredible boor.'–Joan Fontaine

Paul Henreid 'He looks as if his idea of fun would be to find a nice cold damp grave and sit in it.'–Richard Winnington

Katherine Hepburn 'She ran the gamut of emotions from A to B.'–Dorothy Parker on Hepburn's performance in the Broadway play *The Lake*

'Katherine of Arrogance'–sobriquet she acquired at RKO in the 30s

Miriam Hopkins 'Puerile and silly and snobbish . . .'–Edward G. Robinson

'I don't think there was ever a more difficult female in the world.'–Bette Davis (whom some reckoned the second most difficult)

'The least desirable companion on a desert island . . .'–Harvard Lampoon's citation to MH 1940

Alan Ladd 'Alan Ladd is hard, bitter and occasionally charming, but he is, after all, a small boy's idea of a tough guy.'–Raymond Chandler

Burt Lancaster 'Burt Lancaster! Before he can pick up an ashtray, he discusses his motivation for an hour or two. You want to say "Just pick up the ashtray, and shut up!" '–Jeanne Moreau

Vivien Leigh '. . . she made life hell for everybody near her, unless they did everything she wished, as she wished and when she wished.'–Wolfe Kaufman

Jerry Lewis 'One of the most hostile, unpleasant guys I've ever seen . . . arrogant, sour, ceremonial, piously chauvinistic egomaniac.'–Elliott Gould on his childhood idol

Gina Lollobrigida 'Her personality is limited. She is good as a peasant but incapable of playing a lady.'–Sophia Loren

Sophia Loren 'Sophia is a very pretty girl but she cannot threaten me because she is incapable of playing my roles.'–Gina Lollobrigida

Victor Mature 'Hollywood's self-avowed disciple of conceit and vulgarity.'–W. H. Mooring

Marilyn Monroe 'She's just an arrogant little tail-twitcher who's learned to throw sex in your face.'–Nunnally Johnson

'. . . a fat cow.'–Harry Cohn (given what he said about other people, this could be taken as moderately complimentary)

'A professional amateur.'–Laurence Olivier

David Niven '. . . an extremely mean and deeply heartless figure'–fellow actor Peter Willes

Maureen O'Hara 'She looked as if butter wouldn't melt in her mouth–or anywhere else.'–Elsa Lanchester

Mary Pickford '. . . that prissy bitch.'–Mabel Normand

'She was the girl every young man wanted to have–as his sister.'–Allistair Cooke

Ronald Reagan 'Reagan's in the news again. He's at his ranch chopping wood–he's building the log cabin he was born in.'–Johnny Carson

George C. Scott 'A jerk.'–Joseph Levine

Frank Sinatra 'When Frank Sinatra was down he was sweet, but when he got back up he was hell.'–Ava Gardner

'He's the kind of guy that, when he dies, he's going up to heaven and give God a bad time for making him bald.'–Marlon Brando

Barbra Streisand Walter Matthau to BS during filming of *Hello Dolly* (US 69): 'I have more talent in my smallest fart than you have in your entire body.'

'The most pretentious woman the cinema has ever known'–producer Jon Peters

Elizabeth Taylor On herself: 'I have the face and body of a woman and the mind of a child.'

Lana Turner 'She is not even an actress . . . only a trollop.'–Gloria Swanson

Raquel Welch 'Silicone from the knees up.'–George Masters, make-up artist

Orson Welles 'There but for the grace of God, goes God.'–anon on the young Welles

Esther Williams 'Wet she's a star, dry she ain't.'–Fanny Brice

'I can't honestly say that Esther Williams ever acted in an Andy Hardy picture, but she swam in one.'–Mickey Rooney

UNKINDEST CUTS

Verbal annihilation has been the stock in trade of the film critic ever since the very first review. Here are a few intimations that the critic did not think the picture deserved his unqualified approval.

☆ Anthony Slide on Marguerite Duras' *India Song* (Fr 75) 'Without question the most boring, pretentious feature ever foisted on the general public.'

☆ Alan Brien of the Sunday Times on Irwin Allen's *The Swarm* (US 78) '. . . simply the worst film ever made'.

☆ Variety on *The Gong Show Movie* (US 80) 'Bong-g-g-g-g-g.'

☆ Vincent Canby on the $48 million *Inchon* (US/Korea 82) '. . . the most expensive B-movie ever made'.

☆ Variety '*Lonesome Cowboy* is Andy Warhol's best movie to date, which is like saying a three-year-old has graduated from smearing faeces on the wall to the occasional use of finger paints.'

☆ Variety on *Movie Movie* (US 78) 'Awful Awful'.

☆ David Aasen of Newsweek on *A Dream of Passion* (US 78) 'As one endures the spectacle of Mercouri bearing her soul . . . it seems one has wandered into the home movies of a demented culture maven.'

☆ C. A. Lejeune on *No Leave No Love* (US 46) 'No Comment.' (This was the complete review.)

☆ Variety on *The American Prisoner* (GB 29) 'Save for direction, story, dialog, acting and being a period picture, this is a good one.'

☆ The Reporter magazine on *Guess Who's Coming to Dinner* (US 67) 'Abie's Irish Rose in Blackface.'

☆ Anonymous critic on *Cleopatra* (US 63) 'Elizabeth Taylor is the first Cleopatra to sail down the Nile to Las Vegas.'

☆ New York Daily News on *Hawk of Powder River* (US 48) 'Eddie Dean's latest is in black and white rather than color but the improvement is hardly noticeable; you can still see him.'

☆ Judith Crist on *The Agony and the Ecstasy* (US 65) 'All agony, no ecstasy.'

☆ Variety on *Way Back Home* (Belg 81) '. . . so poor that it gives amateurism a bad name'.

☆ Gary Arnold of the Washington Post on Ken Russell's biopic of Tchaikovsky *The Music Lovers* (GB 71) 'Awful . . . the worst experience I ever had in a cinema.'

☆ Variety on *Les Enfants du Paradis* (Fr 44)–which is probably the most universally admired foreign language film of all time '. . . downright dull'.

☆ Colin Bennett of the Melbourne Age on Australia's first sexploitation movie *The Set* (Aus 70) 'At last my 18-year search for the worst film ever made has ended.'

☆ Alan Parker on *The Draughtsman's Contract* (GB 83) '. . . a load of posturing poo poo'.

☆ John Simon on *Camelot* (US 67) 'This film is the Platonic idea of boredom, roughly comparable to reading a three-volume novel in a language of which one knows only the alphabet.'

☆ James Agee on *You Were Meant For Me* (US 48) 'That's what you think.'

ANIMAL ACTS

□□□□□□□□□□□□□□□□□□□□□□□

FELINE FILMS

Dogs have been hogging the screen ever since Cecil Hepworth's *Rescued by Rover* (GB 07) was so successful the negative wore out and the film had to be made all over again. Pussies have never enjoyed the same drawing power, except in cartoons. Here though are 20 movies in which cats have been central to the story line.

☆ *The Black Cat* (US 41) Based on the Edgar Allan Poe story, movie recounts how a flock of relatives of an eccentric old lady who is nuts about cats–she even maintains a cat crematorium–are eagerly awaiting her death so they can inherit. When she is murdered by one of them, they learn that no bequests will be paid until the last of her vast tribe of cats passes on.

☆ *Rhubarb* (US 51) About an alley cat called Rhubarb who inherits $30 million and a major league baseball club.

☆ *The Shadow of the Cat* (GB 61) Cat belonging to murdered woman seems to cause deaths of relatives seeking lost will.

☆ *Puss-in-Boots* (Mex 61) Mexican rendering of the well-loved fairy tale.

☆ *Gay Purr-ee* (US 62) Feature cartoon about a country cat called Mewsette (voice by Judy Garland) who comes to Paris and is kidnapped.

☆ *One Day, a Cat* (Cz 63) Engaging fantasy about a cat who wears glasses and the strange effect on the villagers when he takes them off.

☆ *Three Lives of Thomasina* (GB 63) Thomasina, heroine of a novel by Paul Gallico, is a cat in a small Scottish town who recovers from three crises to the joy of her little mistress, Karen Dotrice.

☆ *Under the Yum Yum Tree* (US 63) Acrobatic feline follows lecherous landlord Jack Lemmon around as he attempts to seduce tenant, Carol Lynley.

☆ *The Incredible Journey* (US 63) Disney movie about a Siamese cat and two dogs, separated from their owner, who cross hundreds of miles of rugged terrain in Canada to return home.

☆ *That Darn Cat* (US 63) Another Disney, in which cat hero helps the FBI solve a case.

That Darn Cat upstaging Hayley Mills.

☆ **Torture Garden** (GB 68) Michael Bryant tangles with a man-eating house cat after greed induces him to permit the death of a supposedly rich relative.

☆ **Eye of the Cat** (US 69) Michael Saarazin as young man with aelurophobia (fear of cats) plotting to do in his wealthy aunt but done in himself by hordes of malign moggies.

☆ **The Aristocats** (US 70) Disney cartoon feature in which two cats are deliberately lost by butler who fears they will inherit his mistress's wealth. Various animal friends restore them to their rightful place.

☆ **The Night of the Thousand Cats** (Mex 72) Demented aristo (Hugo Stiglitz) keeps a thousand man-eating pussies in his castle and feeds them on the flesh of attractive young ladies ill-advised enough to pay a visit.

☆ **Harry and Tonto** (US 74) Art Carney as Harry, old New York widower evicted from apartment, on odyssey across America with cat Tonto.

☆ **I Am a Cat** (Jap 75) A cat observes (via subjective camera) life of teacher in early 20th-century Japan and romantic entanglements of family.

☆ **The Cat from Outer Space** (US 78) Disney fantasy about spaceship commanded by cat forced to make emergency landing on Earth.

☆ **Our Johnny** (Austria 80) Cat called Johnny upsets even tenor of life in humdrum household.

☆ **Cat's Eye** (US 85) Three stories from Stephen King, each involving same cat in bizarre situations.

☆ **The Black Cat** (It 85) Patrick Magee as an experimenter in the paranormal. His cat is suspected by visiting American photographer, Mimsy Farmer, of being the perpetrator of mysterious deaths in an English village.

BIRDS AND BEASTS

The names of God's creatures have been used in so many film titles that this list is confined to titles which consist of solely a bird, fish or mammal name. All belong to dramatic feature films and in the majority of cases the name in the title is metaphorical.

The Albatross (Fr 71)
Alligator (US 80)
The Ape (US 40)
The Bat (US 59)
The Bear (Pol 70)
The Bees (US 78)
Bug (US 75)
The Bushbaby (GB 70)
Butterfly (US 82)
The Cat (Fr 71)
Chameleon (US 78)
The Cobra (It/Sp 68)
Cougar (US 33)
The Cow (Iran 71)
Crab (Ven 82)
The Cricket (US 17)
The Crocodile (Thai 81)
The Deer (Iran 74)
The Dog (Sp 77)
The Doves (Can 72)
The Eagle (US 25)
The Falcon (Yug/W. Ger 81)
The Firefly (US 37)
The Fly (US 55)
The Fox (US 67)
The Frog (GB 37)
The Goat (Fr 82)
The Goldfish (US 24)
The Gorilla (US 31)
Goslings (Cz 81)
The Grasshopper (USSR 55)

The Guinea Pig (GB 48)	*The Raven* (US 63)
The Hen (Fr 33)	*Rhinoceros* (US 74)
The Horse (Tur 82)	*The Rooster* (Israel 71)
The Insect (Jap 64)	*The Salamander* (Swz 71)
Jaguar (US 56)	*The Sandpiper* (US 65)
Kangaroo (US 52)	*The Scorpion* (Neth 84)
The Lamb (US 15)	*The Seagull* (USSR 73)
The Lark (Hu 64)	*Sheep and Mammoths* (Yug 85)
The Leopard (It 63)	*Silkworms* (Sp 76)
The Lizards (It 63)	*Snail* (Israel 70)
Lynx (Pol 81)	*The Spider* (It 70)
The Mole (Mex 71)	*Stork* (Aus 71)
The Moth (Pol 80)	*The Swan* (US 56)
The Octopus (US 15)	*Tawny Pipit* (GB 44)
Orang Outang (Fr 86)	*The Tiger* (Yug 78)
The Peacock (Egypt 82)	*The Trout* (Sp 78)
The Pelican (US 74)	*The Viper* (GB 38)
Penguin (Pol 66)	*The Vixen* (US 16)
Pigs (Eire 84)	*The Vulture* (GB 67)
Piranha (US 78)	*The Wasp* (US 18)
Poodle (Sp 79)	*The Water Spider* (Fr 71)
Praying Mantis (GB 82)	*Wolves* (Hun 74)
Queen Bee (Jap 78)	*The Worms* (Cuba 80)
The Rat (GB 25)	

⌐ □ ⌐

THE NUMBERS GAME

⌐ □ ⌐

BORN BEAUTIFUL ... BUT WHEN?

If there is anything that the stars are more secretive about than their salaries or their lovers, it tends to be their age. Here are some who have sown the seeds of doubt and confusion about their date of birth.

☆ **June Allyson** is variously reported to have been born in 1917 and 1923. The lady herself has never confirmed which.

☆ **Humphrey Bogart** (1899–1957) Bogey was not born on Xmas Day, as Warner Bros publicity liked to claim, but on 23 January.

☆ **James Cagney** (1899–1986) Warner Bros moved his year of birth forward five years to 1904 to exploit his baby-faced appearance.

☆ **Marguerite Clarke** (1881–1940) Like Mary Pickford, she specialised in little girl roles. She continued to play teenagers till she was 40, concealing her real age with a false birth date of 1887.

*Was **The Wicked Lady** 29 or was she 34 in reality?*

☆ **Zsa Zsa Gabor** (1919?) called a press conference to settle the oft speculated question of her age and produced what looked like a genuine birth certificate proving her to be 54 years old. Hollywood columnist Sheilah Graham drily observed that if that was the truth, then Zsa Zsa had married her first husband when she was 13.

☆ **Lillian Gish** (1893) played virgin waifs much given to being beaten by brutal huns and wicked stepfathers. She was not 16 when she made her screen debut, as has generally been supposed, but nearly 20. It was only in 1984, on the occasion of the bestowal of a Life Achievement Award, that the American Film Institute sought out her birth certificate and discovered that in reality she was born in 1893 and not 1896 as hitherto believed. The discovery had a special significance–it made her the first active nonagenarian film star.

☆ **Laurence Harvey** (1928–

73) added a year to his age in order to join the South African Navy when he was still only 14.

☆ **Rock Hudson** (1925–85) His agent added two years to his age to get him more mature parts.

☆ **Margaret Lockwood** The date of her debut in the world is so shrouded in mystery that the doyen of movie reference book writers, Arthur Halliwell, has to fall back on the ambivalent '1911/1916'. Was *The Wicked Lady* 34 or was she only 29?

☆ **Victor McLaglen** (1886–1959) added four years to his age to enlist in the British Army and serve in the Boer War.

☆ **Walter Matthau** (1920) *Who's Who in the Theatre* records his birthdate as 1925. He himself once let slip it was 1920.

☆ **Ann Miller** (1924) is one of the few actresses to have increased her age. She lied about her date of birth to get her first adult film role in ***New Faces of 1937*** (US 37) at age 13, changing 1924 to 1919 to make herself 18. She is still recorded as born 1919.

☆ **Pearl White** (1897–1938) did the same, adding eight years to her age to avoid being cast in the virgin waif roles assigned to the Misses Gish and Pickford. Playing a girl in her mid-20s in ***The Perils of Pauline*** (US 14), she was barely 17 in reality.

HALF CENTURY UP

These are the stars whose movie careers have spanned 50 years or more.

☆ **50 Years**

Melvyn Douglas (1901–81)
Tonight or Never (US 31)
Ghost Story (US 81)

Rex Ingram (1895–1969)
Tarzan of the Apes (US 18)
Journey to Shiloh (US 68)

Gaston Modot (1887–1970)
Onésime (Fr 09)
Les Testaments du Docteur Cordelier (Fr 59)

Pola Negri (1897)
Love and Passion (Pol 14)
The Moonspinners (US 64)

Sir Ralph Richardson (1902–83)
The Ghoul (GB 33)
Give My Regards to Broad Street (GB 85). N B : *Give My Regards to Broad Street* was made in 1983, but not released until two years later.

Michel Simon (1897–1975)
La Vocation d'André Carrel (Swz 25)
The Red Ibis (Fr 75)

☆ **51 Years**

Tullio Carminati (1895–1971)
Il Bacio di Margherita de Cortona (It 12)
Swordsman of Siena (It/Fr 63)

Dorothy Gish (1898?–1968)
An Unseen Enemy (US 12)
The Cardinal (US 63)

Sir Cedric Hardwicke (1893–1964)
Riches and Rogues (GB 13)
The Pumpkin Eater (GB 64)

Curt Jurgens (1912)
Hundert Tage (Ger 35)
Still active 1986

Paul Lukas (1895–1971)
Sphynx (Hun 17)
Sol Madrid (US 68)

Pedro Regas (1892–1974)
debut 1921
High Plains Drifter (US 72)

Ann Sothern (1909)

Broadway Nights (US 27)
The Manitou (US 78)

Nora Swinburne (1902)
Branded (GB 20)
Up the Chastity Belt (GB 71)

☆ **52 Years**

Reginald Denny (1891–1967)
debut 1914
Batman (GB 66)

Isabel Jeans (1891–197?)
The Profligate (GB 17)
The Magic Christian (GB 69)

Bill Kerr (1922)
Harmony Row (US 34)
still active 1986

☆ **Walter Pidgeon** (1897–1984)
Mannequin (US 25)
Sextette (US 77)

☆ **53 Years**

Chester Conklin (1888–1971)
one reel comedies 1913
A Big Hand for a Little Lady (US 66)

Sir Alec Guinness (1914)
Evensong (GB 33)
still active 1986

Bob Steele (1907)
The Adventures of Bill and Bob (US 19)
reported to be playing bit parts 1972

Olga Tschechowa (1896–1980)
Todesreigen (Ger 21)
Freihling auf Immenhof (W. Ger 74)

☆ **54 Years**

James Cagney (1899–1986)
Sinner's Holiday (US 30)
Terrible Joe Moran (US 84)– TVM

Sir John Mills (1908)
The Midshipmaid (GB 32)
still active 1986

☆ **55 Years**

Francis X. Bushman (1883–1966)
Fate's Funny Frolic (US 11)

The Ghost in the Invisible Bikini (US 66)

Bette Davis (1908)
The Bad Sister (US 31)
still active 1986

Stanley Holloway (1890–1982)
The Rotters (GB 21)
Journey into Fear (GB 76)

Cathleen Nesbitt (1888–1982)
The Faithful Heart (GB 22)
Julia (US 77)

Sylvia Sidney (1910)
Broadway Nights (US 27)
Hammett (US 82)

☆ 56 Years

Elizabeth Bergner (1898–1986)
Der Evangelimann (Ger 23)
Whitsun Holiday (W. Ger 79)

Charles Boyer (1899–1978)
L'Homme du Large (Fr 20)
A Matter of Time (It/US 76)

John Carradine (1906)
Tol'able David (US 30)
still active 1986

Fay Compton (1894–1978)
She Stoops to Conquer (GB 14)
The Virgin and the Gypsy (GB 70)

Gladys Cooper (1888–1971)
The Eleventh Commandment (GB 13)
A Nice Girl Like Me (US 69)

Marlene Dietrich (1901)
So Sind die Männer (Ger 22)
Just a Gigolo (W. Ger 78)

Raymond Hatton (1887–1971)
debut 1911
In Cold Blood (US 67)

Mae Marsh (1895–1968)
Man's Genesis (US 12)
Arabella (US 68)

Ray Milland (1905–1985)
The Plaything (GB 29)
The Sea Serpent (It 85)

Sir Laurence Olivier (1907)
Hocus Pocus (Ger 30)
still active 1986

☆ 57 Years

Donald Crisp (1880–1974)
The French Maid (US 06)
Spencer's Mountain (US 63)

Finlay Currie (1878–1968)
The War in the Air (GB 08)
Bunny Lake is Missing (GB 65)

Sylvie (1885–1970)
Britannicus (Fr 12)
Le Ciel des fons (Fr 69)

☆ 58 Years

Minta Durfee (1890–1975)
His Wife's Mistake (US 13)
Willard (US 71)

Myrna Loy (1905)
The Ten Commandments (US 23)–as extra
Summer Solstice (US 81)–TVM

John Stuart (1898–1979)
Her Son (GB 20)
Superman (GB 78)

H. B. Warner (1890–1975)
English Nell (GB 00)
Darby's Rangers (US 58)

☆ 59 Years

Maurice Chevalier (1888–1972)
Trop credules (Fr 08)
Monkeys Go Home (US 67)

Françoise Rosay (1891–1974)
Falstaff (Fr 13)
Pas folie la guêpe (Fr 72)

☆ 60 Years

Lil Dagover (1897–1980)
Harakiri (Ger 19)
Tales from the Vienna Woods (W. Ger/Austria 79)

Fritz Rasp (1891–1976)
Der Phantom (Ger 15)
Lina Braake (W. Ger 75)

Gilbert Roland (1905–1985)
Blood and Sand (US 22)–as extra
Barbarossa (US 82)

Mickey Rooney (1920)
Not to be Trusted (US 26)
still active 1986

Gloria Swanson (1897–1983)
At the End of a Perfect Day (US 14)
Airport 75 (US 74)

Umpei Yokoyama (18??–19??, exact dates unknown)
Inazuma Goto Hobaku no Ba (Jap 99)
still active 1959

☆ *61 Years*

Dame Edith Evans (1888–1976)
A Welsh Singer (GB 15)
Nasty Habits (GB 76)

Douglas Fairbanks Jr (1909)
Party Girl (US 20)
Ghost Story (US 81)

☆ *62 Years*

Sir John Gielgud (1904)
Who Is the Man? (GB 24)
still active 1986

☆ *65 Years*

Margit Makay (1892)
Bitter Love (Hun 12)
A Very Moral Night (Hun 77)

☆ *68 Years*

Bessie Love (1898–1986)
The Flying Torpedo (US 15)
The Hunter (US 83)

Cyril Cusack (1910)
Knocknagow (Ire 18)
still active 1986

☆ *70 Years*

Charles Vanel (1892)
Jim Crow (Fr 12)
still active 1982

Ruth Gordon (1896–1985)
Camille (US 15)
Maxie (US 85)

☆ *72 Years*

Francesca Bertini (1888–)
La Dea del Mare (It 04)
1900 (It 76)

☆ **Curt Bois** (1900–)
Mutterliebe (Ger 09)

The Boat Is Full (Swz 81)

☆ *73 Years*

Helen Hayes (1900)
Jean and the Calico Doll (US 10)
A Caribbean Mystery (US 83)– TVM

☆ *74 Years*

Lillian Gish (1893)
An Unseen Enemy (US 12)
still active 1986.

THE ONE AND ONLY

☆ **The only film seen by less people than appeared in it** was the last Nazi epic *Kolberg* (Ger 45), released in January 1945 at a time when few Berlin cinemas were still operating. The total audience was rather less than the prodigious cast of 187,000, which included whole army divisions diverted from the front on Goebbels' orders.

☆ **The only western directed by a woman** was Ruth Ann Baldwin's oddly titled Universal production *'49–'17* (US 17).

☆ **The only stuntman who doubles for child actors** is 4 ft 9 ins Bobby Porter, who substitutes for little girls as well as little boys. He it is and not 9-year-old Aileen Quinn you see suspended from a 20-storey high drawbridge in *Annie* (US 82).

☆ **Britain's only sexually segregated cinema** was the Gem at Great Yarmouth. When it opened in 1908, the local council decreed that men and women should not sit together.

☆ **The only full-length feature film made without a camera** was Barcelona artist Jose Antonio Sistiaga's remarkable 75-minute animated one-man production *Scope, Colour, Muda* (Sp 70). Completed in 17 months between October 1968 and February 1970, it was painted frame by frame direct on to the film stock by Sistiaga single-handedly.

☆ **The only outright ban on a particular individual** being represented in Hollywood films applied to gangster John Dillinger, whose heroic stature in the mass consciousness had considerably unnerved the US authorities by the time he was gunned down in 1934. For ten years the censors would consider no scripts featuring him, though eight Dillinger movies have been made since 1945.

☆ **The only film on which production began *after* the death of the star was Blake Edwards'** *The Trail of the Pink Panther* (GB 82), starring Peter Sellers (1925–80) as Inspector Clouseau. The story was knit together with clips and out-takes from five earlier Pink Panther movies, plus linking shots with an uncredited lookalike filmed from a distance or heavily disguised, and flashbacks to Clouseau's youth using a couple of child actors. The result was considered so appalling by Sellers' widow, Lynne Frederick, that she sought and won a multi-million dollar settlement for infringement of her late husband's contractural rights.

☆ **The only studio that was also a municipality** was Universal City. Opened in 1915, it really was a city–with a City Hall, a fire station and its own police force under the command of America's first woman police superintendent.

☆ **The only film with an orchestral accompaniment composed entirely of stringed instruments** was Alfred Hitchcock's *Psycho* (US 60). Hitchcock wanted music that would help to chill the audience to a high pitch of terror. Composer Bernard Herriman responded with what he described as a black-and-white sound to complement a black-and-white film of a black-and-white story.

☆ **Hungary is the only country in which film appreciation** is part of the regular school curriculum.

☆ **The only film with a cast composed entirely of method actors** was *The Strange One* aka *End As a Man* (US 57). Among the graduates of New York's Actors' Studio in the picture were Ben Gazzara, George Peppard, Mark Richman, Pat Hingle, Arthur Storch, Julie Wilson, Paul Richards, Geoffrey Horne, James Olson and James Wilson.

☆ Rumours of 'snuff movies', exploitation pictures in which a performer is supposed to be done to death, abounded in the early 1970s but proved unfounded. There is, however, **one film in which performers are seen being killed in reality.** In the final battle sequence of the anti-British propaganda film *Mein leben für Irland* (Ger 41), several extras were killed when one stepped on a live land mine and the footage was retained in the release prints.

☆ **Britain's only cinema for blacks** was opened in Cardiff in 1935. Admission was 1d.

☆ **The only film in which the leading players met for the first time on camera** was Jon

Jost's **Slow Moves** (US 84), about two strangers thrown into a close relationship. The director deliberately kept Roxanne Rogers and Marshall Gaddis apart to capture the authenticity of their first meeting.

☆ **The only British monarch to have acted in films was King Edward VIII** when he was Prince of Wales. He appeared in three feature films, each time playing himself: two in 1919–**The Power of Right** and **The Warrior Strain**–and one in 1927, BIP's **Remembrance**, a story about disabled war veterans.

☆ **The only film with an all-male cast to be directed by a woman** was Ida Lupino's **The Hitch-Hiker** (US 53).

☆ **The only museum in the world devoted to home movies** is the Buckingham Movie Museum. It also boasts the only cinema in the world where patrons can select the film they would like to see.

☆ **The only full-length feature film made in sign language** for the deaf was Peter Wechsburg's **Deafula** (US 75), a horror movie about Dracula's illegitimate son.

☆ **There has been one western in which not a single gunshot is heard**–**They Passed This Way** aka **Four Faces West** (US 48), starring Joel McCrea as a bank robber on the run from Charles Bickford's Pat Garrett. It bombed at the box office.

☆ **The only film ever released in Britain under two different titles simultaneously** was **This England** (GB 41), a wartime flag-waver starring Emlyn Williams and Constance Cummings, which became **Our Heritage** north of the border.

☆ **The only instance of the same score being used for two different films** was in the case of Alfred Newman's music for MGM's **The Prisoner of Zenda** (US 37), which was repeated in quickened tempo for the 1951 remake.

☆ **The only occasion brothers have played the same role in different movies** was when Don Ameche was cast in the title role of **The Story of Alexander Graham Bell** (US 36) and his brother Jim Ameche as Bell in **The Story of Mankind** (US 57). There has also been one occasion when brothers took the same role in the same movie–twins Anthony and David Meyer playing the Prince interchangeably in **Hamlet** (GB 78).

☆ **The only film shot without the stars knowing they were in it** was Sergei Komorov's **The Kiss of Mary Pickford** (USSR 26). During the visit of Mary Pickford and Douglas Fairbanks to Moscow in July 1926, Komorov posed as a newsreel cameraman and followed them around shooting enough footage to piece together a full-length comedy feature after their departure. It was an engaging tale of a film extra who is determined to kiss 'the world's sweetheart'–and succeeds! Most remarkable of all was the climatic sequence of the close embrace between Soviet hero and Hollywood heroine. Although the film has now been shown publicly in the west, no one has been able to offer an explanation of how Komorov managed to contrive this scene.

☆ **The only film starring Siamese twins** was a low budget exploiter titled **Chained for Life**

(US 31), with Daisy and Violet Hilton.

☆ Many movies have been based on magazine short stories, but **only once have two movies been derived from stories published in a single issue of a magazine.** *Bringing Up Baby* (US 38), with Cary Grant and Katherine Hepburn, was based on the story by Hagar Wilde; while John Ford's classic *Stagecoach* (US 39) was from Ernest Haycox's *Stage to Lordsburg*. Both appeared in the 10 April 1937 issue of *Collier's*.

☆ **The only Hollywood leading lady who never kissed her leading man on screen** was Chinese-American star Anna May Wong. She nearly achieved it in *The Road to Dishonour* (GB 29); indeed her kissing scene with John Longden was actually shot, but it was cut by the censor on the grounds that inter-racial love would be offensive to some patrons.

☆ **The only feature film in which the frame of the picture changed to allow any shape** that suited the action was *The Door in the Wall* (GB 56). Made in the Dynamic Frame process, the configuration of the scenes ranged from a narrow slit to a large square.

☆ **The only recorded case of a film being hijacked** occurred in Dublin in 1925, when a band of terrorists removed the current release at the Masterpiece cinema, a patriotic British war film titled *Ypres*, at gunpoint. The Manager succeeded in obtaining another print, whereupon the same terrorists blew up the cinema to prevent it being shown.

☆ **The only country never to have imposed film censorship** is Belgium.

☆ **The only ex-slave to have made a name in pictures** was Harry Gray, who was born in North Carolina twenty years before Lincoln's proclamation of emancipation, and first appeared on screen at the age of 86 as the parson in the pioneer all-black talkie *Hallelujah!* (US 29).

☆ **The only Hollywood movie ever shown on Soviet TV** was *They Shoot Horses, Don't They?* (US 69), starring Jane Fonda. The story of a dance hall marathon set in the Depression, it gave a sufficiently unflattering view of America to be considered ideologically sound for Russian viewers.

☆ **The only feature film which runs backwards** is *Happy End* (Cz 68), with all the characters walking backwards, food emerging from mouths, a guillotined head joining the body (opening shot) etc. Dialogue is forwards as far as the structure of the words is concerned, but responses come before the questions they answer.

☆ **The only 'Son of . . .' film to star 'the son of'** was *Son of Captain Blood* (US 62), with Sean Flynn in the title role. His father Errol had starred in *Captain Blood* (US 35).

PICK A NUMBER

Number One (US 69)
Two for the Road (GB 67)
These Three (US 36)
Four Daughters (US 38)
Five Star Final (US 31)
Six of a Kind (US 34)

Seven Brides for Seven Brothers (US 54)
Eight Bells (US 35)
Hook and Ladder No 9 (US 27)
Ten Laps to Go (US 38)
Oceans Eleven (US 60)
12 Hours to Kill (US 60)
13 Fighting Men (US 60)
The 14 (GB 73)
15 Yok Yok (Thai 78)
Night of Jan 16 (US 41)
Number 17 (US 21)
Hangar 18 (US 80)
19 Red Roses (Den 74)
Bar 20 (US 43)
Girls Under 21 (US 40)
What Happened at 22 (US 16)
23 Paces to Baker Street (US 56)
24 Eyes (Jap 60)
25 Fireman's Street (Hun 74)
Occupation in 26 Pictures (Yug 78)
27 Down Bombay–Varanasi Express (India 74)
28 Up (GB 85)
Twenty-Nine (GB 69)
Hurry Up, or I'll Be 30 (US 73)
Adalen 31 (Swe 69)
I Lived Under Thirty Two Names (Hun 72)
A Woman of 33 (Bul 83)
Fire on East Train 34 (USSR 84)
Otokowa Tsuraiyo No. 35 (Jap 85)
36 Hours to Kill (US 36)
37.2 Degrees in the Morning (Fr 86)
Only 38 (US 23)
The 39 Steps (GB 35)
Life Begins at 40 (US 35)
1941 (US 79)
Der 42 Himmel (Swz 63)
Shell 43 (US 16)
44 or Tales of the Night (Mor 85)
45 Fathers (US 37)

Here the sequence breaks, as no one has yet made a movie with the number 46 in the title.

🎬🎬🎬🎬🎬🎬🎬🎬🎬🎬🎬🎬🎬🎬🎬🎬🎬🎬🎬🎬🎬🎬

CO-STAR COUNT

The record for the most appearances as co-stars is held by India's Prem Nazir and Sheela, who have made 130 films together. Hollywood's co-starring teams have rather more modest scores:

☆ **Jill Ireland** and **Charles Bronson**–14 films

☆ **Myrna Loy** and **William Powell**–13 films

☆ **Janet Gaynor** and **Charles Farrell**–12 films

☆ **Sophia Loren** and **Marcello Mastroianni**–12 films

☆ **Lila Lee** and **Thomas Meighan**–11 films

☆ **Ginger Rogers** and **Fred Astaire**–11 films

☆ **Judy Garland** and **Mickey Rooney**–10 films

☆ **Katherine Hepburn** and **Spencer Tracy**–10 films

☆ **Jeanette MacDonald** and **Nelson Eddy**–8 films

☆ **Greer Garson** and **Walter Pidgeon**–8 films

☆ **Olivia de Havilland** and **Errol Flynn**–8 films

🎬🎬🎬🎬🎬🎬🎬🎬🎬🎬🎬🎬🎬🎬🎬🎬🎬🎬🎬🎬🎬🎬

RECORDS

☆ **The longest first-run of a film in one cinema** was for **Emmannuelle** (Fr 74), which was seen by 3,268,874 patrons during the 10 years and 32 weeks it ran at the Paramount City cinema in Paris between June 1974 and February 1985.

☆ **The greatest age span portrayed by a single actor** in a film was by 33-year-old Dustin Hoffman, who played the title role of *Little Big Man* from the age of 17 to 121.

☆ **The longest any Hollywood actor was under contract to a single studio** was 29 years in the case of Lewis Stone, best remembered for his portrayal of Judge Hardy in the Andy Hardy films. He became a MGM contract artiste at the studio's inception in 1924 and remained with them until his death in 1953.

☆ **The star who has received the most fan mail during the 1980s** is Bo Derek, with up to 50,000 letters a week.

☆ **The largest movie set** was the 1,312 ft × 754 ft Roman Forum built on a 55 acre site near Madrid for Samuel Bronston's *The Fall of the Roman Empire* (US 64). The highest elevation, the roof of the Temple of Jupiter, reached 260 ft above the paving of the Forum.

☆ **The smallest movie set** was built for *Bill and Coo* (US 47), which was filmed entirely in a model village mounted on a 30 ft × 15 ft table. The performers were love birds.

☆ **The greatest age at which anyone has embarked on a regular movie career** was 84 in the case of miniscule 4 ft 9 in character actress Lydia Yeamans Titus. She made her screen debut in the Rudolph Valentino film *All Night* in 1918 and played in over 50 features before her death in 1929 at the age of 95.

☆ **The foreign star with the highest ever rating at the US box office** was Brigitte Bardot, who was seventh in 1958.

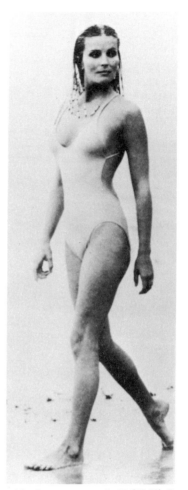

*After her appearance in **10** (US 79), Bo Derek was receiving a record 50,000 fan letters a week.*

☆ **The youngest star to have topped the list of box office draws in the US** was 7-year-old Shirley Temple in 1935. The oldest was 64-year-old Marie Dressler in 1933.

☆ **The highest jump without a parachute by a movie stuntman** was 232 ft by A. J. Bakunas, doubling for Burt Reynolds, in *Hooper* (US 78). He fell onto an air mattress.

☆ **The longest non-stop cinema show** was a 50-hour 'B Movie Marathon' which took place at the Variety Arts Center in Hollywood on 29–31 May 1983. Tickets were $15 to see 37 low-budget classics.

☆ **The biggest selling record of a song from a movie** is *White Christmas*, performed by Bing Crosby in *Holiday Inn* (US 42), which has sold over 30 million copies to date.

☆ **The largest assemblage of assorted animals in a movie** totalled 8,552 in *Around the World in Eighty Days* (US 56), to wit: 3,800 sheep; 2,448 buffalo; 950 donkeys; 800 horses; 512 monkeys; 17 bulls; 15 elephants; 6 skunks; 4 ostriches.

☆ **The greatest number of retakes of a single scene** was 342 for the sequence in Chaplin's *City Lights* (US 31) in which the blind flower girl (Virginia Cherrill) sells the little tramp a flower in the mistaken belief he is a wealthy tycoon. Chaplin kept reshooting because he could not think of a satisfactory way of making the girl think he was rich.

☆ **Hollywood's youngest director of all time** was Sam Raimi, who helmed his debut film *The Evil Dead* (US 82) at the age of 19. The oldest was George Cukor, who was 81 when he was signed for *Rich and Famous* (US 81) with Candice Bergen and Jacqueline Bisset.

☆ **Hollywood's youngest producer of all time** was Steven Paul, who produced and directed the Elliott Gould, Susannah York

romance *Falling in Love Again* (US 80) at the age of 20.

☆ **The busiest ever Hollywood star**, in terms of movies completed during a limited period of time, was comedienne Joan Blondell, who played in 32 feature films in only 27 months between 1930 and 1933.

☆ **The Hollywood star who played the most leading roles** was John Wayne, who appeared in 153 movies from *The Drop Kick* (US 27) to *The Shootist* (US 76). In all but 11 of these he played the lead.

☆ **The star who has made the most films of all** is the Indian comedienne Manorama, who made her screen debut in 1958 and completed her 1,000th film in 1985. Of the total, 999 were in Tamil and one in Hindi (a language she does not speak). Manorama works on as many as 30 films at the same time.

☆ According to a survey conducted by *TV Guide*, **the movie most often repeated on American television** is *Casablanca* (US 42), with *King Kong* (US 33) second. *King Kong* had a head start over the rest of the contenders–it was the first picture from a Hollywood major to get a release on TV when the studios began to abandon their vendetta against the upstart medium in 1956.

☆ **The largest number of foreign films released in the USA** in any one year was 361 in 1964. The number of domestic releases was 141. The lowest number of foreign films was 30 in 1943, against 397 Hollywood productions.

☆ **The record for seeing the**

most films is held by Albert E. Van Schmus, who viewed a total of 16,945 during his 32 years as a rater for the Motion Picture Association of America between 1949 and 1982.

☆ **The youngest performer to receive star billing** was Leroy Overacker, known on screen as Baby Leroy, who was chosen at age 6 months to play opposite Maurice Chevalier in *Bedtime Story* (US 33). His grandfather had to sign the contract, because not only was the star under age, but so was his 16-year-old mother. Baby Leroy is fondly remembered by movie buffs as the infant whose milk was allegedly spiked with gin by the child-hating W. C. Fields.

☆ **The longest screen kiss** occupies 3 min 5 sec of Regis Toomey's and Jane Wyman's time in *You're In the Army Now* (US 40).

☆ **The shortest shooting schedule of all time** was one day for Paul Vecchialli's 80-minute feature film *Trou de Memoire* (Fr 85). Starring Francoise Lebrun and Vecchialli himself, the picture was shot with film stock left over from a documentary he had been commissioned to make.

☆ **The lowest fee paid for the script of a major Hollywood feature** was the $10 earned by Preston Sturges for *The Great McGinty* (US 40). Sturges was a scriptwriter who wanted to direct. The deal with Paramount was that he should be given the opportunity in return for doing the script for a nominal fee.

☆ **The fictional character most often portrayed on screen is Sherlock Holmes**, who has been played by 68 different actors in 187 films between 1900 and 1986.

☆ **The historical character most often represented on screen is Napoleon Bonaparte**, portrayed in 177 films between 1897 and 1986.

☆ **The largest screen ever used for projecting a motion picture** was the 115 ft × 85 ft (35 m × 26 m) installation at the Tsukuba Expo '85 in Japan, on which a 20 minute $2 million production *Skywards* (Can 85) was presented by the Canadian Imax system. The largest ever video screen, the 131 ft × 82 ft (40 m × 25 m) Sony Jumbotron, featured at the same exhibition.

☆ **The greatest destruction of crockery in a film** occurred in *Little Nightingale* (USSR 36), the story of a revolt of women workers in a porcelain factory on the Volga, in which 150,000 plates were shattered.

☆ **The highest paid executive in Hollywood** is Barry Diller, chairman of 20th Century Fox and its parent TCF Holdings, whose annual salary on appointment in October 1984 was set at $3 million. In addition, his five year contract allows him 25% of any increase in the value of the equity of the company, plus 17.5% of any increase during the three years following the termination of his contract.

☆ **The most video swamped city in the world** is Bombay, with 15,000 video libraries–over three times the UK total of 4,500. In addition there are 500 'vid parlours' where people can watch video movies.

☆ **The city with the fewest cinemas** in relation to its population is Cairo with ten for 12 million inhabitants. (Jedda has none, but movies are illegal in

Three of the 68 actors who have played Sherlock Holmes: Top left *Basil Rathbone and Nigel Bruce in* **The Hound of the Baskervilles** *(US 39)* Top right *Arthur Wotner in* **Silver Blaze** *(GB 37)* Above *Christopher Plummer and James Mason in* **Murder by Decree** *(GB/Can 79).*

Saudi Arabia.)

☆ **The longest delay between the completion of a movie script and the making of the movie** was 32 years in the case of **The Doctor and the Devils** (GB 86). The script, about the Edinburgh grave robbers Burke and Hare, was written by the Welsh poet Dylan Thomas for the Rank Organization in 1954 and was finally brought to the screen by Brooksfilm.

☆ **The largest production crew on a movie** consisted of the 556 craftsmen and technicians employed by producer Suketaru Taguchi on Kon Ichikawa's 2½ hr documentary **Tokyo Olympiad** (Jap 65). The largest number on a dramatic feature was 532 for the British World War I flying story **Gunbus** (GB 86).

Many other movie records are contained in *The Guinness Book of Film Facts and Feats.*

COMIC STRIP CHARACTERS

A host of comic strip characters have been portrayed on screen in live action feature-length movies. This list is confined to English language films. The name following the abbreviation 'Orig' is that of the originator of the comic strip.

☆ Zorro holds a number of records. The black-garbed Robin Hood of Southern California was the first comic strip character to be the subject of a major feature film, in **The Mark of Zorro** (US 20) with Douglas Fairbanks; the fastest to make it from strip to screen–the film appeared only the year after the comic strip; and is the strip character most often portrayed on screen–in no less than 68 movies to date. Orig: Johnston McCulley.

☆ Ginger Meggs, cartoon larrikin in Australian newspapers, was played by Ray Griffin in **Those Terrible Twins** (Aus 25). Orig; James Bancks.

☆ **Ella Cinders** (US 26) with Colleen Moore. Orig: William Counselman and Charles Plumb.

☆ Fatty Finn, an urchin of the backstreets of Sydney, was played by 'Pop' Ordell in **The Kid Stakes** (Aus 26). Orig: Syd Nicholls.

☆ **Tillie the Toiler** (US 27) with Marion Davies as the office girl heroine. Orig: Russ Westover in the *New York American*.

☆ **Harold Teen** (US 28) with Arthur Lake. Orig: Carl Ed.

☆ J. Farrell MacDonald played Jiggs and Polly Moran played Maggie in **Bringing Up Father** (US 28). Orig: George McManus.

☆ **Skippy** (US 30) with Jackie Cooper. Orig: Percy Crosby.

☆ **Sooky** (US 31) with Robert Coogan in the name part and Jackie Cooper as Skippy. Orig: Percy Crosby.

☆ **Little Orphan Annie** (US 32) with Mitzi Green. Orig: Harold Gray and Al Lowenthal.

☆ **Harold Teen** (US 34) with Hal LeRoy. Orig: Carl Ed.

☆ **Tailspin Tommy** (US 34) with Maurice Murphy as the young flying ace. First serial based on comic strip. Orig: Hal Forrest.

☆ **Palooka** (US 34) with Stuart Erwin. Orig: Ham Fisher.

☆ **Flash Gordon** (US 36) with Buster Crabbe. Serial. Orig: Alex Raymond.

☆ **Jungle Jim** (US 37) with Grant Withers. Serial. Orig: Alex Raymond.

☆ **Tim Tyler's Luck** (US 37) with Frankie Thomas. Serial. Orig: Lyman Young.

☆ **Blondie** (US 38) with Penny Singleton in the title role and Arthur Lake as Dagwood. First of a series of 28 supporting features made by Columbia 1938–50. Orig: Chic Young.

☆ **Little Orphan Annie** (US 38) with Ann Gillis. Orig: Harold Gray and Al Lowenthal.

☆ **Flash Gordon's Trip to Mars** (US 38) with Buster Crabbe. Serial. Orig: Alex Raymond.

☆ **Dick Tracy Returns** (US 38) with Ralph Byrd. Serial. Orig: Chester Gould.

☆ **Tracy's G-Men** (US 39): as above.

☆ John Trent as Tailspin Tommy

in **Sky Patrol** (US 39). Serial. Orig: Hal Forrest.

☆ **Buck Rogers** (US 39) with Buster Crabbe. Serial. Orig: Dick Calkin.

☆ **Li'l Abner** (US 40) with Granville Owen. Orig: Al Capp.

☆ **Adventures of Captain Marvel** (US 41) with Tom Tyler. Orig: C. C. Beck.

☆ **Tillie the Toiler** (US 41) with Kay Harris. Orig: Russ Westover.

☆ **Private Snuffy Smith** (US 42) with Bud Duncan. Orig: Billy de Beck.

☆ Bud Duncan as Snuffy Smith in **Hillbilly Blitzkrieg** (US 42). Orig: Billy de Beck.

☆ **Winslow of the Navy** (US 42) with Don Terry. Serial. Orig: Lt Com Frank Martinek.

☆ **Dixie Dugan** (US 43) with Lois Andrews. Orig: Joseph McEvoy. In this case McEvoy's strip had itself been based on a film–**Show Girl** (US 28).

☆ **Dick Tracy** (US 45) with Morgan Conway. Orig: Chester Gould.

☆ **Joe Palooka, Champ** (US 46) with Joe Kirkwood, who also starred in eight other Palooka movies 1947–51. Orig: Ham Fisher.

☆ Joe Yule as Jiggs and Renie Riano as Maggie in **Bringing Up Father** (US 46); also in **Jiggs and Maggie in Society** (US 48) and **Jiggs and Maggie Out West** (US 50). Orig: George McManus.

☆ **Dick Tracy vs Cueball** (US 46) with Morgan Conway. Orig: Chester Gould.

☆ **Dick Tracy's Dilemma** (US 47) and **Dick Tracy Meets Gruesome** (US 47) with Ralph Byrd. Orig: Chester Gould.

☆ **Jungle Jim** (US 48) with Johnny Weissmuller in this and seven other Columbia low budgeters. Orig: Alex Raymond.

☆ **Bomba the Jungle Boy** (US 49) with Johnny Sheffield; first of series of 12 which continued to 1955. Orig: Roy Rockwell.

☆ **The Adventures of Jane** (GB 49) with Christabel Leighton-Porter. Orig: Norman Pett.

☆ Scotty Beckett as Corky and Jimmy Lydon as Skeezix in **Gasoline Alley** and **Corky of Gasoline Alley** (both US 51). Orig: Frank O. King.

☆ **Superman and the Mole Men** (US 51) with George Reeves. Orig: Jerry Siegel.

☆ **Blackhawk** (US 52) with Kirk Alyn. Orig: Reed Crandall and Charles Guidera.

☆ **Prince Valiant** (US 54) with Robert Wagner. Produced in colour and Cinemascope, this was the first major motion picture of the talkie era to be based on a comic strip. Orig: Harold Foster.

☆ **The Sad Sack** (US 57) with Jerry Lewis. Orig: George Baker.

☆ **Li'l Abner** (US 59) with Peter Palmer. Orig: Al Capp.

☆ **Dondi** (US 61) with David Kory. Orig: Gus Edson and Irwin Hasen.

☆ **Modesty Blaise** (GB 66) with Monica Vitti in title role and Terence Stamp as Willie Garvin. Orig: Peter O'Donnell and Jim Holdaway.

☆ **Batman** (US 66) with Adam West in title role and Burt Ward as

Robin. Orig: Bob Kane.

☆ *Barbarella* (Fr/It 67) with Jane Fonda. Orig: Jean-Claude Forest.

☆ *The Adventures of Barry McKenzie* (Aus 72) with Barry Crocker; sequel *Barry Mackenzie Holds His Own* (Aus 74). Orig: Barry Humphries–the only comic strip artist to have appeared in the films based on his strip.

☆ *Tiffany Jones* (GB 73) with Anouska Hempel. Orig: Pat Tourret and Jenny Butterworth.

☆ *Friday Foster* (US 75) with Pam Grier, based on first comic strip with black heroine. Orig: Jorge Longaron.

☆ *Superman* (GB 78) with Christopher Reeve; followed by *Superman II* (GB 81) and *Superman III* (GB 84). The first in the series is claimed to have been the most expensive film ever made. Orig: Jerry Siegel.

☆ *Spider-man Strikes Back* (US 78) and *The Dragon's Challenge* (US 80) with Nicholas Hammond. Orig: Stan Lee.

☆ *Buck Rogers* (US 79) with Gil Gerard. Orig: Dick Calkins.

☆ *Fatty Finn* (Aus 80) with Ben Oxenbould. Orig: Syd Nicholls.

☆ *Flash Gordon* (GB 80) with Sam J. Jones. Orig: Alex Raymond.

☆ *Conan the Barbarian* (US 82) with Arnold Schwarzenegger. Orig: Robert E. Howard.

☆ *Annie* (US 82) with Aileen Quinn as Little Orphan Annie. Orig: Harold Gray and Al Lowenthal.

☆ *Ginger Meggs* (Aus 82) with Paul Daniel. Orig: James Bancks.

IT COULD ONLY HAPPEN IN HOLLYWOOD

OVER THE TOP

☆ When he made his super-extravagant *The Merry-Go-Round* (US 23), director Erich von Stroheim attired the guardsman extras in pure silk underclothes monogrammed with the emblem of Austria's Imperial Guard. Von declared that, though the garments were not visible, they helped the players to feel that they belonged to the Austria-Hungary of the Hapsburgs.

☆ In 1931, as the soup queues of America grew ever longer, cowboy star Tom Mix spent $1,000 on white sombreros.

☆ When lesbian producer/actress Nazimova starred in her own production of *Salome* (US 23), she employed only gay actors as a 'homage' to Oscar Wilde.

☆ Gloria Swanson was known as 'the second woman in Hollywood to earn a million dollars and the first to spend it'. (The first millionairess, Mary Pickford,

made sure she held on to it.)
Among Miss Swanson's outgoings
was the cost of having an
expensive tiled floor laid out at her
home specially for Rudolph
Valentino to perform a tango on.
Another was that she never wore
the same dress twice.

☆ During her brief and
tempestuous stay in Hollywood in
the 1930s, French siren Simone
Simon walked off the set at Fox
Studios in a rage and told
production chief Darryl Zanuck: 'I
must have a panther. I like to have
wild things around me–and he'll
look beautiful when I take him
shopping with me.'

☆ Many stars have lost their
trousers in comedies: Oliver Reed
lost his for real in 1978 when he
was found staggering down a
Toronto thoroughfare in shirt-tails,
his legs exposed to the icy winds
of a Canadian winter afternoon.

☆ Hollywood's oriental superstar
of the silent era, Sessue
Hayakawa, owned a gold-plated
Pierce-Arrow–until Fatty Arbuckle
acquired one exactly similar. Then
Sessue gave his away to the Long
Island Fire Department.

☆ Shirley Temple received
135,000 gifts on her 8th birthday.

☆ Rudy Vallee tried to have the
name of the street where he lived
in the Hollywood Hills changed to
Rue de Vallee. When neighbours
banded together to resist the
proposal, he described them as 'a
bunch of disgruntled pukes'. Cecil
B. DeMille had more clout. He
lived in the Hollywood Hills at
2010 DeMille Drive.

☆ The ballroom of the Palace of
Versailles built by MGM for **Marie
Antoinette** (US 38) was larger
than the magnificent 17th century
original built by the 'Sun King',
Louis XIV.

☆ Clara Bow had her limousine
painted to match the colour of her
flaming red hair and rode around
Hollywood in it accompanied by
two Chows whose fur was dyed
the same hue.

☆ During the making of
Cleopatra (US 63), Elizabeth
Taylor's then husband Eddie
Fisher was paid $1,500 a day to
make sure she got to work on
time.

☆ William Randolph Hearst gave
orders that every Hearst
newspaper was to mention the
name of his mistress and
protogee, Marion Davies, at least
once in every issue. The
instruction was carried out for 30
years, long after Miss Davies had
retired from the screen, but was
rescinded within 24 hours of
Hearst's death in 1951.

☆ Silent screen star Francis X.
Bushman kept 300 Great Danes on
his California estate.

☆ At Rudolph Valentino's
notorious 'lying in state' after his
premature death in 1926, the bier
was flanked by Black Shirt guards
who gave the fascist salute and
one of the largest and gaudiest
wreaths read 'from Benito'.
Neither had anything to do with
the Italian government–guards
and wreath had both been
arranged by press agents for
Campbell's Funeral Home.

☆ On a visit to Cuba in the 1930s,
Errol Flynn hired a full orchestra to
follow him wherever he went
playing a constant serenade.

☆ Engaged to star in *Mame* on the
London stage, Ginger Rogers
arrived in England with 118 pieces

of luggage. Wisely she came by ship.

☆ Howard Hughes spent nearly $12 million trying to buy up every surviving print of his disastrous box office flop *The Conquerer* (US 56). The film had cost $6 million to produce.

☆ Fan dancer Sally Rand, who made her movie debut in 1924, was still dancing in the nude as a grandmother in her mid-70s. And she still had the 35–22–35 figure that had enchanted audiences 50 years earlier.

☆ 'Country Boy' Charles Ray specialised in portrayals of simple rustics down on the farm. His off-screen home life was somewhat different–all the door knobs in his Beverly Hills mansion were made of solid gold. He and his wife dressed for dinner every night of the year, whether there were guests or not. The good times did not last and Ray ended his career as an extra.

☆ Esther Ralston, blonde star known as 'the Paramount Clotheshorse', was wont to be driven round Hollywood in a Rolls Royce by a chauffeur whose livery would always match the colour of the dress she was wearing.

☆ Cecil B. DeMille was so determined to ensure the accuracy of *Cleopatra* (US 34) that he despatched art director William Cameron Menzies to Egypt to find out the real colour of the pyramids–all of them. Menzies and his aides visited 92 pyramids at a cost of $100,000. His report to DeMille was that the pyramids are the colour most people suppose them to be–sandy brown. (The film was in black-and-white.)

☆ Ramon Novarro commanded his house guests to wear only black, white and silver, to match the black fur and silver decor of his Frank Lloyd Wright designed mansion.

☆ Buster Keaton owned 20 cars, all at once. The most opulent was 30 ft long and had sleeping accommodation for six, two drawing rooms, a kitchen and an observation deck. Built to resemble a yacht, the vehicle was 'captained' by Buster dressed in an admiral's uniform.

☆ Rin Tin Tin was the only dog in America with a valet, a personal chef, his own limousine and a chauffeur for his exclusive use. He also had a five-room dressing room complex of his own on the studio lot.

☆ After the success of *Gone With the Wind* (US 39) had confirmed legendary status (at least in Hollywood) on David O. Selznick, the newly-minted mogul modestly suggested to his publicity chief that a major university should be invited to confer an honorary doctorate on him. When it was reported to Selznick that no major institution of learning could be persuaded to fall in with the plan, Selznick is alleged to have responded: 'Well, find two minor universities who will give me a degree. I'll be satisfied with that.'

CINEMA CINEMA

A prodigious number of movies have been made about the business of movie making, from *Merton of the Movies* to *A Star is Born* and beyond. Not many movies have the showing of films as a central theme. Here are the few which do.

☆ **Playbox Adventure** (GB 36) Enid Stamp Taylor as heiress who works as ticket seller in cinema.

☆ **Contraband** (GB 40) Michael Powell-Emeric Pressburger production about spies using cinema as a front.

☆ **The Smallest Show on Earth** (GB 57) Bill Travers and Virginia McKenna as young couple who think they have inherited a luxury picture palace, but find that it is in fact a run-down little flea-pit. Charming story recounts how they make it pay (e.g. turning the heat up during desert movies and then selling iced drinks).

☆ **Targets** (US 68) Peter Bogdanovich's second movie, in which a crazed sniper terrorises the audience of a drive-in. Notable for Boris Karloff's last major performance.

☆ **The Projectionist** (US 70) A projectionist fantasises he is Captain Flash under the baleful eye of tyrant cinema manager.

☆ **The Last Picture Show** (US 71) Peter Bogdanovich's evocation of small town life in Texas c. 1950, with the single cinema as the main centre of entertainment and social intercourse.

☆ **The Picture Show Man** (Aus 77) Rivalry between two travelling picture shows in backblocks Australia of 1920s.

☆ **The Enchanted Sail** (It 82) Two brothers take a travelling cinema wagon round rural Italy in 1920s.

☆ **Variety** (US 83) Set in a sex cinema called Variety, in which the box office girl finds herself being drawn to events on screen and becomes entangled with one of the patrons.

☆ **Mr Love** (GB 85) Barry Jackson as cinema projectionist in Southport who plays Bogey live on stage to the usherette's Bergman when the projector breaks down during **Casablanca**.

☆ **American Drive-In** (US 85) Rare example of a film in which the whole of the action takes place in a cinema–in this case a hick town drive-in during the showing of a double bill of **Hard Rock Zombies 1** and **2**. Mainly a study of audience types, including a biker gang, a hooker, two little old ladies who turn out to be dope dealers, and an intellectual couple who earnestly analyse the hokum on screen.

☆ **The Purple Rose of Cairo** (US 85) Woody Allen's ultimate movie fantasy, in which the fictional hero of a topper and tails 30s society movie walks out of the screen to romance unhappily married working girl and besotted movie fan Mia Farrow.

☆ **Demons** (It 85) Horror movie set in cinema showing horror movie.

PROPS

☆ Johnny Mack Brown used William Bonney's own gun when he played the title role in **Billy the Kid** (US 30). Wild Bill Hickock's vest pocket Deringer was a prop in **The Iron Horse** (US 24).

☆ The golden spike which united the Union Pacific and Central Pacific Railroads at Promontory Point, Utah, in 1869 was used for the reconstruction of the episode in **Union Pacific** (US 39).

☆ The telephone Harpo Marx ate in **The Coconuts** (US 29) was made of chocolate and the bottle of ink he drank was Coke.

☆ For the cornfield scene in **Oklahoma!** (US 55) where Gordon Macrae sings that 'the corn is as high as an elephant's eye', the producers engaged an agricultural specialist to grow corn for them to a skyscraping 16 ft. They need not have bothered. The eye of a full-grown elephant is only 8 ft from the ground.

☆ The only western hero to smoke a pipe in his films was Tim Holt.

☆ The bugle blown to sound the charge of the Light Brigade was blown again for the charge scene in **Balaclava** (GB 28).

☆ The props list for **Gone With the Wind** (US 39) contained 1,250,000 items.

☆ The green vomit that gushed out of Linda Blair in **The Exorcist** (US 73) was realistic enough to make some viewers throw-up themselves. It was in fact only a simple concoction of split pea soup and oatmeal.

☆ Geraldine Farrar's armour in **Joan the Woman** (US 16) was made of pure silver. This was not Hollywood extravagance writ large, but a practical solution to the weight problem–silver was the lightest durable metal prior to the widespread availability of aluminium.

☆ At first the custard pies used in slapstick comedies were the real thing, but it was soon found that they had a distressing tendency to disintegrate in the air. A patisserie

called Greenberg's in Glendale, Calif, came up with a solution to the problem–a special ballistic custard pie with a double thickness of pastry and a filling of flour, water and whipped cream. The filling came in two flavours: blackberry if the recipient was a blonde, lemon meringue for a brunette.

☆ The Emperor Franz Josef's golden coach in Von Stroheim's **Merry-Go-Round** (US 22) was the real thing.

☆ The raindrops in **Singin' in the Rain** (US 52) had milk added so that they would register better on film.

☆ The boots eaten by Charlie Chaplin in **The Gold Rush** (US 24) were made of licorice,

☆ During the early 1950s, when television was beginning to make heavy inroads into the motion picture business, MGM banned any use of television sets as props in their films.

☆ James Stewart has kept every hat he has worn in movies since his debut in **The Murder Man** (US 35).

☆ The despatch box used by Abraham Lincoln during his Presidency was loaned by the US Government for use in Selig's Civil War drama **The Crisis** (US 16).

☆ When MGM auctioned off a 45 year accumulation of props and costumes in 1970, Judy Garland's size 4½ shoes from **The Wizard of Oz** (US 39) were knocked down to a lawyer called Richard Wonder for $15,000. It was hardly flattering to Sophia Loren that her bloomers from **Lady L** (Fr/It/US 65) should fetch no more than a mere $50.

☆ The largest land-based prop

ever constructed for a movie was the 60 ft long, 40 ft high Wooden Horse of Troy used in Robert Wise's **Helen of Troy** (US 54). It weighed 80 tons and 30 full grown trees and over 1,000 lbs of nails were needed to build it. A modern air conditioning system was fitted to save the 25 occupants from heat prostration.

☆ Ned Kelly's bullet-proof helmet and jerkin, fashioned from ploughshares, was borrowed from the Victoria museum and worn by the actor playing the famous bushranger in the world's first full-length feature film, **The Story of the Kelly Gang** (Aus 06).

☆ Gore can occasionally be real. The severed horse's head placed in an unfortunate character's bed in **The Godfather** (US 71) was not faked–it was flesh and quite a lot of blood.

☆ The most valuable assemblage of props ever to be brought together on a single set was the $10 million worth of paintings and sculptures used for the art gallery scenes in Universal's **Legal Eagles** (US 86). They included works by Willem De Korning, Roy Lichtenstein, Alexander Calder and Pablo Picasso.

☆ The most expensive single prop ever used on a movie was the full scale replica of a Spanish galleon built for Roman Polanski's **Pirates** (US/Tun 86) at a cost of £7 million. Designed by Pierre Guffrey, its construction kept 2,000 Maltese shipyard workers in jobs for a whole year.

UNUSUAL CASTS

☆ The only feature length film with a cast composed entirely of American Indians was **The Silent Enemy** (US 30).

☆ There have been two films with all-Eskimo casts, **Kivalina of the Ice Lands** (US 25) and **Igloo** (US 32), and three Hollywood movies with all-Balinese casts–**Virgins of Bali** (US 32); **Goona-Goona** (US 32) and **Legond, Dance of the Virgins** (US 32). One American film has been made with an all-Siamese cast, **Chang** (US 27); and one with an all-Sudanese cast, **Stampede** (US 30).

☆ Two films have had an all-Maori cast, **Romance of Hine Moa** (NZ 29) and **The Devil's Pit** (NZ 29). The Italian film **Zeliv** (It 28) had an all-Zulu cast.

☆ In **Sitting Bull** (US 54), the Indians and the US Cavalry were all played by Mexicans. In Samuel Fuller's war picture **Big Red One** (US 80), all the Nazi concentration camp guards were played by Jews.

☆ **The Writing on the Wall** (Fr/Belg 82) was a story of the Northern Ireland troubles in which all the Protestants were played by Catholics and the Catholics by Protestants.

☆ Nearly all the performers in **Amy** (US 81) were deaf–they were recruited from the California School for the Deaf at Riverside. Mentally handicapped actor Richard Mulligan was cast as the most brilliant and intellectual teacher on campus in the off-beat high school social comedy, **Teachers** (US 84). The title role in **Annie's Coming Out** (Aus 84), based on a true story about a brain damaged teenager, was played by real-life spastic Tina Arhondis.

☆ Members of the International Brigade played in André Malraux's **Man's Hope** (Sp 45), filmed from his own novel during the bombardment of Barcelona in 1938. For three allied fliers who were shot down over Switzerland in World War II, not only was it the end of their war but the opportunity to star in a film. John Hoy and E. G. Morrison of the RAF and Ray Reagan, USAAF sergeant, were given the leading roles in the Swiss film **Last Chance** (Swz 45), playing escaped prisoners leading a party of refugees over the Alps to neutral Switzerland. The refugees, all of different nationalities, were played by real refugees.

☆ All the leading players in **Dionysus** (Fr 84), about a US university professor who comes to Paris to defend a thesis on Dionysus and ends up running an assembly line at Citroen, were played by real life university professors.

☆ Beauty queens have often been given a chance to break into movies, but never so many all at once as in **Yankee Pasha** (US 54). A costumer about a New England girl sold into a Moroccan harem, the cast included the Misses USA, Japan, Panama, Norway, Uruguay, South Africa, Australia and Miss Universe, Christiane Martel.

☆ RKO tried an unusual experiment in 1944 with a film called **Days of Glory** (US 44), in which all 19 featured players were making their screen debut. One of the 19 went on to stardom– Gregory Peck.

☆ Von Stroheim used real

hookers to play the prostitutes in **The Wedding March** (US 27) and similarly the inmates of the bordello in John Huston's **Under the Volcano** (US 85) were real-life members of their calling. Not so in **Maya** (Fr 49). A set representing a red light district was built in false perspective to give an illusion of depth. The prostitutes seen at the far end of the street were played by little girls of 6 to 8 years old outfitted in the gaudy raiment of harlotry.

☆ The masochists receiving the punishing attentions of Bulle Ogier in **Maitresse** (Fr 79) were not actors. They were deviants who were invited to bring along their own chains and whips.

☆ The extras engaged to play convicts in **Hell's Highway** (US 32) were all ex-cons themselves.

☆ There have been many prison dramas and war films with all male casts, but very few films with all-female casts. Best known is probably **The Women** (US 39), whose 135 speaking roles included those played by Joan Crawford, Norma Shearer, Rosalind Russell, Paulette Goddard and Joan Fontaine. Others have been: **Maedchen in Uniform** (Ger 31) with Dorothea Wieck; **The Mad Parade** (US 31) with Evelyn Brent; **The Bitter Tears of Petra von Kant** (W. Ger 72) with Margit Carstensen; **Cries and Whispers** (Swe 72) with Harriet Andersson, Ingrid Thulin and Liv Ulmann; and **Friendships, Secrets and Lies** (US 79) with Sondra Locke, Tina Louise and Paula Prentiss.

☆ Equally rare are films with all-child casts. There have been two in which the children are playing children: Peter Brook's **The Lord**

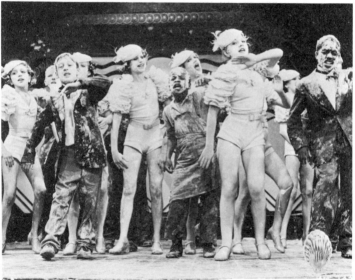

Top *Peter Brook's **The Lord of the Flies** had an all-child cast, but it was definitely not a film for children.* Above *The only musical with an all-child cast– Alan Parker's gangster spoof **Bugsy Malone**.*

of the Flies (GB 63), from William Golding's novel about schoolboy castaways on an uninhabited island who revert to barbarism; and *Leave Us Alone* (Den 75), which had a similar theme of children adapting to life on a desert island. In addition there have been three films in which children play adults. **General Spanky** (US 37), starring Spanky McFarland of Our Gang fame, was a burlesque melodrama of the Civil War, while **Bugsy Malone** (GB 76) parodied the gangster movies of the 30s with a then unknown Jodie Foster as a 13-year-old femme fatale. The cast of **The Annunciation** (Hun 84), in which Adam, the first man, is guided through the darker passages of man's tormented history, were all between 8 and 12, with the part of Satan played by a 9-year-old girl.

☆ There have been isolated examples of children playing adults in straight dramas. Blanche Sweet played a married woman at the age of 13 in **A Man with Three Lives** (US 09) and 12-year-old Gladys Leslie took the role of a debutante in **The Beloved Imposter** (US 19). Mickey Rooney played an adult midget in **Orchids and Ermine** (US 27) at the age of 7 and this led to a persistent rumour that the child star was in reality a midget posing as a child. The reverse principle, of adults playing children, was not uncommon in silent days, when actresses like Mary Pickford and Lillian Gish specialised in such roles. More unusual examples are the 33-year-old Richard Barthelmess playing a 6-year-old boy in the opening scenes of **The Little Shepherd of Kingdom Come** (US 28) and Bette Davis's portrayal of a 13-year-old in **Payment on Demand** (US 51) when she was 43.

☆ To round off the subject of diminutive performers, there have been two films with all-midget casts: a western called **The Terror of Tiny Town** (US 38) and Werner Herzog's **Even Dwarfs Started Small** (W. Ger 70).

☆ Veteran producer Mario Cecchi Gori assembled a mammoth cast for his 125th picture **The Department Store** (It 86) which included every available performer who had appeared in his previous 124 films.

STATESMANLIKE PERFORMANCES

Ronald Reagan is by no means the only leader of his country to have acted in movies. These are the other statesmen, politicians and rulers who have done so.

☆ **Lady Astor**, first woman MP to take her seat in the House of Commons, as herself in **Royal Cavalcade** (GB 35).

☆ **Godfrey Binaisa**, President of Uganda, played bit parts in **King Solomon's Mines** (US 50) and **The African Queen** (GB 51).

☆ **Sir David Brand**, Premier of Western Australia, played himself in **Nickel Queen** (Aus 71).

☆ **Fidel Castro**, Cuban dictator, played bits in **Holiday in Mexico** (US 46) and other Hollywood films with a Latin-American setting.

☆ **Josephus Daniels**, US Secretary to the Treasury, played himself in **Victory** (US 13).

☆ **Jimmie Davis**, Governor of Louisiana, played himself in the autobiopic **Louisiana** (US 47).

☆ **Moshe Dayan**, Israeli Minister of Defence, played himself in **Operation Thunderbolt** (Israel 77).

☆ **Georgi Dimitrov**, Prime

Minister of Bulgaria after World War II, played himself in **Kampfer** (USSR 36).

☆ **King Edward VIII** played himself as the Prince of Wales in **The Power of Right** (GB 19), **The Warrior Strain** (GB 19) and **Remembrance** (GB 27).

☆ **Michael Foot**, leader of the Labour Party, played himself in **Rockets Galore** (GB 58).

☆ **John Gorton**, Prime Minister of Australia, played himelf in **Don's Party** (Aus 76).

☆ **John Hodge**, Minister of Pensions, played himself in **Broken in the Wars** (GB 19).

☆ **William Morris Hughes**, Prime Minister of Australia, played himself in **Smithy** (Aus 46).

☆ **Hubert Humphrey**, US Senator, played himself in **The Candidate** (US 72).

☆ **Jomo Kenyatta**, President of Kenya, played an African chief in **Sanders of the River** (GB 35).

☆ **John Lindsay**, Mayor of New York, played Senator Donnovon in **Rosebud** (US 75).

☆ **George McGovern**, US Senator, played himself in **The Candidate** (US 72).

☆ **Benito Mussolini** was an extra in Famous Players' **The Eternal City** (US 14).

☆ **Ignace Paderewski**, Prime Minister and later President of Poland, played himself (in his better known role of concert pianist) in **Moonlight Sonata** (GB 37).

☆ **Kukrit Pramoj**, Prime Minister of Thailand (1974), played the Prime Minister of the fictitious state of 'Sarkhan' in **The Ugly American** (US 62).

☆ **Yizhak Rabin**, Prime Minister of Israel, played himself in **Operation Thunderbolt** (Israel 77).

☆ **Marudur Gopelan Ramechandran**, Chief Minister of Tamil Nadu (formerly Madras), is South India's foremost superstar. Known to fans as 'M.G.R.', he plays swashbuckling heroes who protect the poor from their oppressors, a role he seeks to emulate in his political life.

☆ **N. T. Rama Rao**, Chief Minister of Andhra Pradesh (1983), is one of the Indian screen's matinee idols.

☆ **Theodore Roosevelt**, President of the USA 1901–09, played himself in **Womanhood, The Glory of a Nation** (US 17); is also claimed to have appeared in unidentified one-reel comedy starring Matty Roubert in 1914.

☆ **Prince Sihanouk**, Cambodia's Head of State before the communist takeover, was a prolific director and also starred in **Twilight** (Cam 69) and **Storm Over Angkor** (Cam 69).

☆ **Franz von Trauberg**, first post-war Mayor of Berlin, played the kidnapped ambassador in **Guernica** (It 72).

☆ **Leon Trotsky**, USSR Commissar for War and founder of the Red Army, played Russian nihilists in **My Official Wife** (US 14) and **The Battle Cry of Peace** (US 15).

☆ **Gough Whitlam**, Prime Minister of Australia, as 'man in nightclub' in **The Broken Melody** (Aus 38) and as himself in **Barry McKenzie Holds His Own** (Aus 74).

DID YOU KNOW THAT ...

☆ The scene in **The Public Enemy** (US 31) where James Cagney screws a grapefruit in Mae Clarke's face, was originally intended to be played with an omelette. When the script was changed to make the weapon a grapefruit, director William Wyler assured her that the scene would be faked. It wasn't. Cagney not only gave her a zinger with the fruit, he twisted it so hard it made her nose bleed.

☆ Another film in which the violence was real was **The Pledgemasters** (US 71), about the hazing of candidates for a college fraternity. Four student volunteers, playing the 'pledges', were subjected to force feeding until they vomited, made to do exercises until they collapsed from exhaustion, and savagely beaten with a razor strop. No special effects were used.

☆ Tom Kelly's celebrated nude shot of Marilyn Monroe netted the calendar company $750,000. MM was paid $50.

☆ The most popular Hollywood actress in China is Deborah Raffin. This is on the strength of a TVM titled **Nightmare in Badham County** (US 77), one of the few American films released in China, which has been seen by over 200 million Chinese.

☆ At her death from leukaemia in 1969, former skating star Sonja Henie was one of the ten wealthiest women in the world.

☆ It is now more common for British households to have a video recorder than to take a holiday abroad or own a freezer. According to a 1985 survey, more is spent on video casettes than on overcoats, wholemeal bread, yogurt, flour, household tools, cinema visits ... or underpants.

☆ Both Tyrone Power Sr and Tyrone Power Jr died on the set; the father while making **The Miracle Man** (US 32) and the son while making **Solomon and Sheba** (US 59).

☆ Elsa Lanchester's make-up for the title role in **The Bride of Frankenstein** (US 35) was so rigid that she had to be fed lunch through a tube.

☆ A thousand nuns rioted in Seoul in 1983 in protest against a film called **Buddhist Nun's Story** (S. Korea 83). They claimed that 20 of the 199 scenes were too sexually explicit.

☆ Pushy mothers are endemic in Hollywood, but few could hold a candle to the formidable parent of Allen Clayton Hoskins, who dressed her son up as a girl to audition for the part of Farina in the **Our Gang** comedies. For as long as he remained in the series, the unfortunate Master Hoskins had to remain in drag–and play his role well enough off-screen for producer Hal Roach not to twig.

☆ Ronald Reagan did a sensible thing giving up movies for an alternative career. Otherwise they might have given him up. In his last movie, Universal's **The Killers** (US 64), he was billed fourth, below Lee Marvin, Angie Dickinson and John Cassavetes. It was the first and only time he played the heavy, a role that even ardent supporters of the Democratic Party would have to concede was casting against type.

☆ Rosemary De Camp, who played James Cagney's mother in **Yankee Doodle Dandy** (US 42), was 14 years younger than her screen 'son'.

☆ Pressure from the Italian-American League succeeded in having the word 'Mafia' wholly eliminated from the script of **The Godfather** (US 71). (It was rumoured they made the producers an offer they couldn't refuse.)

☆ The fastest draw in the west isn't a western star at all, but a comic–Jerry Lewis. His time to clear leather, cock and fire his pistol is 35/100ths of a second–rather quicker on the draw than the swiftest western star, Clint Eastwood, whose best time is 45/100ths of a second. Incidentally the fast draw is wholly a movie phenomenon. It was not important in the real Old West, where the usual practice was to shoot your opponent nice and slowly–in the back.

☆ When the Russian classic **The End of St Petersburg** (USSR 27) was released in America, the chamber of commerce of St Petersburg, Florida, complained that it would ruin their tourist business.

☆ In 1985 Bette Davis donated 59 scrapbooks to Boston University library. Still a matter of speculation among library staff is why in a picture of Joan Crawford all her teeth have been blacked out.

☆ Hollywood has played host to actors of nearly all nationalities, but there was only ever one Eskimo who made a successful career in Tinsel Town. It may have helped, Hollywood being Hollywood, that Mala (his screen name) enjoyed the unusual distinction of being a Jewish Eskimo.

☆ Carmen Miranda's career was brought to a premature finish when it was revealed that she wore no panties under her skirt. The deficiency was a practical one; it gave her more freedom of movement when she danced. Unfortunately on one occasion a freelance stills photographer who was on the set took some pictures from a very low angle. They revealed all. The shots were circulated clandestinely and women's morality groups hounded 20th Century Fox into dropping her option.

☆ Only 20% of the films aired on BBC1 are British, whereas domestic product accounts for nearly 47% of the films shown on ITV. (Based on 1984 figures.)

☆ In 1936 it was reported that Robert Woolsey, the bespectacled half of RKO's Wheeler and Woolsey comedy team, had consumed 20,000 cigars in the course of screen and publicity work. In real life he was a non-smoker.

☆ Marion Davies was only 14 when she was taken under the protection of 50-year-old newspaper magnate William Randolph Hearst early in 1914.

She was a chorus girl, two years under the legal age, in **The Movie Queen** at the Globe Theatre in New York.

☆ Frederico Fellini's distinguished actress wife Giulietta Masina accepted a role in **The Mad Woman of Chaillot** (GB 69), one of the few films not directed by her husband in which she has appeared. She did so for the best of reasons: to get Katherine Hepburn's autograph.

☆ When Bela Lugosi died in 1956 he was buried in Dracula's cloak.

☆ There is one scene in **Oliver Twist** (GB 48) in which Fagin is played not by Alec Guinness, who happened to be unavailable the day it was shot, but by the director, David Lean.

☆ The world's only nursery for the children of working film actresses–open 24 hours a day–is the Estancia Infantil in Mexico City. It was founded by Mexico's most famous Hollywood star, Dolores Del Rio. Actresses can leave their children there for weeks or months while they are on location.

☆ In Thibodaux, Louisiana, there were two cinemas before World War II. The larger was the Grand. Its smaller rival was the Baby Grand.

☆ A lot of people know that there was a fifth Marx called Zeppo, but how many are aware of the sixth one–Frenchie Marx? He was in one film, **Monkey Business** (US 31), in an unbilled role.

☆ A picture of the infant Bogart, sans sneer, was used to advertise Mellin's Baby Food.

☆ Studios were seldom made to eat humble pie, least of all by the stars they owned, but Warner Bros met its match in Jane Wyman, the then Mrs Ronald Reagan. Jack Warner disliked her film **Johnny Belinda** (US 48) so much that he sacked director Jean Negulesco and refused to release it. When eventually it got a showing, the critical acclaim was unanimous. And when the movie scored ten Oscar nominations, Jane Wyman forced Jack Warner to take a trade ad apologising to cast and crew.

☆ Another who got her own back was Lucille Ball, whose full potential as a whacky comedienne was never realised by RKO; they put her into a series of indifferent pictures in the 30s and 40s. She is the only star to have secured the ultimate revenge on a Hollywood studio–by buying it up. In 1957 she took over RKO Studios for her TV production company, Desilu. Under her own management, she was to find success in the very place where it had eluded her for 20 years.

☆ Michael Cimino shot 220 hours of film for his $57 million epic **Heaven's Gate** (US 81) to produce a release print which one critic described as 5 hours 25 minutes of 'staggering self-indulgence'. When the long version flopped, it was cut to 2½ hours.

☆ Kay Thompson's mischievous heroine of the *Eloise* series of children's books is said to have been based on the young Liza Minnelli. Disney's Peter Pan was modelled on Bobby Driscoll, who also did the voice, while Tinkerbell in the 1953 cartoon feature was based on Marilyn Monroe. Earlier he had chosen dancer Marge Champion as the model for Snow White in his first feature-length cartoon film, **Snow**

White and the Seven Dwarfs
(US 37), and Bela Lugosi on which to base Tchernobog the Black God in *Fantasia* (US 40). The original of the comic book hero Captain Marvel was none other than Fred MacMurray, who must have appeared in more heroic stature in early youth than the amiable but somewhat shambling figure of later years. Another comic strip artist who looked to Hollywood for inspiration was Milton Caniff, creator of *Terry and the Pirates*, whose villainous Dragon Lady in that long-running adventure was his incarnation of Joan Crawford at her wickedest.

☆ Mae Clarke, whose movie immortality was assured the moment James Cagney pushed a grapefruit in her face in *The Public Enemy* (US 31) (see above), was the original inspiration for another immortal, the daffy Lorelei Lee in Anita Loos' 1926 novel *Gentlemen Prefer Blondes*, a role played by June Walker in the original stage version and by Ruth Taylor and Marilyn Monroe in the 1928 and 1953 movie versions respectively. Anita Loos encountered Mae in 1924–long before she entered movies–when she was a 'cute little blonde' being squired around town by literary critic H. L. Mencken.

☆ The world's only blind film producer is Bombay-based Bhupat Giri, who made his production debut with *Bhed Bhav* (Ind 85). Back in 1920 in Ireland a film called *Rosaleen Dhu* was filmed by a blind cameraman.

☆ Rod Cameron married his own mother-in-law. His third wife was Angela Alves-Lico; his fourth her mother.

☆ The real-life Baron Franckenstein (with a 'c'), a professional actor, appeared in *Young Frankenstein* (US 74) under his screen name Clement St George, though not as his namesake.

☆ Louis B. Mayer, notwithstanding the advice of MGM studio executives, refused to put aspiring cartoon maker Walt Disney under contract in 1928 after seeing a preview of the first Mickey Mouse movie because he thought that pregnant women would be frightened of a ten foot high rodent on the screen.

☆ An Italian dictionary contains the word *Lollobrigidian*. It is defined as 'a landscape with prominent hills'.

☆ Marlon Brando has fathered a son by both the actresses who played Fletcher Christian's Tahitian lover in the 1935 and 1962 versions of *Mutiny on the Bounty*. Morita Castenda, in the 1935 version, was his second wife; Tarita, who played opposite him in the '62 version, was his lover both on and off screen.

☆ Black Brazilian soccer ace, Pele, not only starred in the film of his own life-story *Pele* (Mex 78), he composed the score as well.

☆ Nudity reached the Chinese screen in 1985 with a picture called *The Rickshaw Boy*. A girl was seen totally naked–but from the rear only.

☆ Maud Adams has the distinction of being the only 'Bond Girl' to have appeared in two Bond movies. She made her screen debut in *The Man With the Golden Gun* (GB 74) and nine years later appeared in *Octopussy* (GB 83). The only performer to have been cast in all UA's Bond films is Canadian actress Lois Maxwell who, in the person of M's secretary, Miss Moneypenny, continues to suffer from unrequited love for 007.

☆ Humphrey Bogart was buried with a small gold whistle. It was placed in the coffin by his wife, Lauren Bacall, as a tribute to their life together on screen and off. It recalled her line to him when she made her debut in *To Have and Have Not* (US 44): 'If you want anything, just whistle . . .'

☆ Only one man in Germany saw Chaplin's *The Great Dictator* (US 40), a savage satire on the Nazi dictatorship. The film was banned outright, but on Hitler's personal orders a print was obtained through neutral Portugal and in total seclusion the Führer viewed it not once but twice.

☆ The pooch in the title role of *The Magic of Lassie* (US 77) was the great-great-great grandson of the original Lassie (actually a male Collie called Pal) who debuted in *Lassie Come Home* (US 42) with the young Elizabeth Taylor.

☆ Gussie Berger, Emily Clark, Jane Emerson, Mary Holmquist and Karin Lund were all one and the same person: Garbo incognito. Charles Bogle, Otis Cribecoblis, Mahatma Kane Jeeves, Primrose Magoo, Felton J. Satchelstern and Ampico J. Steinway also shared a single identity: W. C. Fields, sometimes as screenwriter, other times to conceal a new bank account.

☆ Clarence Nash (1904–85), the immortal voice of Donald Duck, may have been incomprehensible quacking in his native American, but he could be equally hard on the ear in French, Spanish, Portuguese, Japanese, German and Chinese. None of these languages could he understand– Nash had the words written out phonetically and gabbled them in Duckspeak for the delight of audiences from Paris to Pekin.

HAPPY CHRISTMAS

I'll Be Seeing You (US 44) shell-shocked soldier (Joseph Cotten) is sent on furlough by his doctor to prove he can face the world again and meets a girl on a train (Ginger Rogers) on parole from gaol who invites him to her aunt's for Xmas.

Christmas in Connecticut (US 45) Barbara Stanwyck as a single lady who writes for a housekeeping magazine and invents a husband, child, farm and ability to cook to satisfy stern, moralistic publisher (Sydney Greenstreet). When he asks her to take in a sailor on leave for Xmas, and decides to come too, she is obliged to borrow a farmhouse and a husband.

Miracle on 34th Street (US 47) Edmund Gwenn as inmate of old folks' home who takes on a

Santa Claus job at Macy's and encounters moppet (Natalie Wood) who does not believe in S.C. By the end he has convinced not only the sceptical child, but a hard-boiled New York judge as well.

Bush Christmas (GB 47) Chips Rafferty adventure story about children riding home through Australian bush for Xmas holiday who fall among horse thieves.

Christmas Eve (US 47) Ann Harding as an eccentric old lady trying to find her three adopted sons, grown-up and scattered, to bring them together at Christmas and save the estate from her scheming nephew (Reginald Denny).

Who Killed Santa Claus (Fr 48) Harry Baur as village toymaker who dresses up as Santa every year to bring presents to all the children. A gold ring used in the Christmas mass is stolen and an unknown man is found murdered in the Santa Claus outfit.

O Henry's Full House (US 52) Episodic film of O. Henry's short stories, including *The Gift of the Magi*. Poor young couple (Jeanne Crain and Farley Granger) each sacrifices a prized possession to buy a Xmas gift for the other–she sells her long hair to buy him a fancy watch fob; he sells his watch to buy a silver comb for her beautiful tresses.

The Holly and the Ivy (GB 52) Country vicar (Ralph Richardson) learns the truth about the wayward members of his family as they gather together for Christmas.

The Crowded Day (GB 54) Events in a day at a department store during the Xmas

*Bing Crosby starred in what is probably the most known of all the Xmas movies, **White Christmas**.*

rush. With John Gregson, Rachel Roberts, Thora Hird, Dora Bryan.

White Christmas (US 54) Bing Crosby and Danny Kaye as old army buddies, now a musical team, who trek to Vermont for a white Christmas at their old general's holiday inn and pull him out of a financial hole by putting on a show.

All Mine to Give (US 56) 12-year-old boy (Rex Thompson) tries to find homes for his smaller brothers and sisters on Xmas Day after death of widowed mother (Glynis Johns) the day before.

Santa Claus (Mex 59) Joseph Elias Moreno as a Mexican Santa Claus from outer space.

Santa Claus Has Blue Eyes (Fr 66) Jean-Pierre Leaud as small town youth whose casual employment as a Santa Claus photographic model opens up new opportunities.

The Christmas Tree (GB 66) Adventures of three children

taking a Xmas tree across London to a hospital.

Santa and the Three Bears (US 70) Cartoon feature about bear cubs in Yellowstone National Park who put off hibernation in order to see Santa Claus–even when their mother admonishes them 'You've stayed up a month past your bedtime.'

The Christmas Martian (Can 71) E.T. type story about a friendly Martian who lands in northern Quebec at Xmas time and is taken care of by two children. Resembles E.T. even to the final chase and escape of the Extra-Terrestial.

The Passions of Carol (US 75) Porno version of Dickens' *A Christmas Carol*.

The Night Before Christmas (It 78) Italian film set in London with Christopher George and Gay Hamilton as separated couple reunited on Christmas Eve as their child lies dying of a rare disease.

Criminal Conversation (Eire 80) This title is the Irish legal term for adultery. On Xmas Eve two couples meet to celebrate, but during the course of the evening it is revealed that one of the husbands has been having an affair with the other's wife.

Santa Claus is a Louse (Fr 82) Comedy about the oddball characters who phone a counselling service on Xmas Eve.

Bush Christmas (Aus 82) Remake of 1947 film (see above).

A Christmas Story (US 83) About a young boy in the 1940s who wants an air rifle for Christmas above everything else in the world. Starring Melinda Dillon.

Don't Open Till Christmas (GB 84) Edmund Purdom as a detective tracking down a maniac (Alan Lake, husband of Diana Dors) who is killing Santa Clauses all over London.

Christmas Present (GB 85) Spirited Christmas fable about brash young director of old fashioned City bankers who is entrusted with traditional seasonal task of delivering a Christmas gift to a poor deserving family.

One Magic Christmas (US/Can 85) 6-year-old moppet faces miserable Xmas with Dad made redundant and Mom in despair until angel (Harry Dean Stanton) takes her on magical trip to visit Santa Claus (Jim Rubes).

Santa Claus (US 85) David Huddleston plays Santa, and Dudley Moore the chief elf in charge of his toy workshop, in $50 million moppet pic which relates how Santa first arrived at the North Pole and what happened when he lit out for New York City.

Note There have also been versions of Dickens' *A Christmas Carol* in 1901, 1913, 1914, 1916, 1935, 1938, 1950, 1970 and 1972, besides the porno version noted above.

...AND FINALLY

A COMPLETE LIST OF ALL THE HOLLYWOOD ACTRESSES WHO HAVE PUBLICLY DECLARED THEIR VIRGINITY

☆ **Brooke Shields**